The Dances of
Shakespeare

The Dances of Shakespeare

Written and
Illustrated by

Jim Hoskins

ROUTLEDGE
NEW YORK AND LONDON

Published in 2005 by
Routledge
Taylor & Francis Group
270 Madison Avenue
New York, NY 10016

Published in Great Britain by
Routledge
Taylor & Francis Group
2 Park Square
Milton Park, Abingdon
Oxon OX14 4RN

© 2005 by Taylor & Francis Group, LLC
Routledge is an imprint of Taylor & Francis Group

Printed in the United States of America on acid-free paper
10 9 8 7 6 5 4 3 2 1

International Standard Book Number-10: 0-415-97434-8 (Softcover)
International Standard Book Number-13: 978-0-415-97434-9 (Softcover)
Library of Congress Card Number 2005001699

Library of Congress Cataloging-in-Publication Data

Hoskins, Jim, 1934-
    The dances of Shakespeare / by Jim Hoskins.
        p. cm.
    Includes bibliographical references and index.
    ISBN 0-415-97434-8 (pbk. : acid-free paper)
    1. Shakespeare, William, 1564-1616--Dramatic production--Handbooks, manuals, etc. 2. Shakespeare, William, 1564-1616--Knowledge--Dance--Handbooks, manuals etc. 3. Dance--History--16th century--Handbooks, manuals, etc. 4. Dance--History--17th century--Handbooks, manuals, etc.
    I. Title.

PR3091.H66 2005
822.3'3--dc22   2005001699

Taylor & Francis Group
is the Academic Division of T&F Informa plc.

Visit the Taylor & Francis Web site at
http://www.taylorandfrancis.com

and the Routledge Web site at
http://www.routledge-ny.com

Dedicated to the memory of
Lowell Manfull

TABLE OF CONTENTS

PROLOGUE

SIR ANDREW: I am a fellow o' th' strangest mind i' th' world. I delight in masques and revels sometimes altogether.

SIR TOBY: Art thou good at these kickshawses, knight?

SIR ANDREW: As any man in Illyria, whatsoever he be, under the degree of my betters, and yet I will not compare with an old man.

SIR TOBY: What is thy excellence in a galliard, knight?

SIR ANDREW: Faith, I can cut a caper.

SIR TOBY: And I can cut the mutton to 't.

SIR ANDREW: And I think I have the back-trick simply as strong as any man in Illyria.

SIR TOBY: Wherefore are these things hid? Wherefore have these gifts a curtain before'em? Are they like to take dust, like Mistress Mall's picture? Why dost thou not go to church in a galliard and come home in a coranto? My very walk should be a jig. I would not so much as make water but in a sink-a-pace. What dost thou mean? Is it a world to hide virtues in? I did think, by the excellent constitution of thy leg, it was formed under the star of the galliard.

Twelfth Night, or, What You Will, Act 1, scene iii

Another test of an actor's physical control was in dancing. Apart from the dances written into the actual texts of the plays, it was usual to end the performance with a dance performed by some of the members of the company. A traveller from abroad who saw Shakespeare's company act *Julius Caesar* said that "when the play was over they danced very marvelously together," and when the English actors travelled abroad, special mention was always made of their ability as dancers. The fashion of the time was for violent, spectacular dances and the schools in London taught intricate steps like those of the galliard, the exaggerated leap called the "capriole" and the violent lifting of one's partner high into the air that was the "volte." A visitor to one of these dancing schools of London watched a performer do a galliard and noted how "wonderfully he leaped, flung and took on"; and if amateurs were talented at this kind of work, professionals on the stage were expected to be very much better.

Shakespeare of London by **Marchette Chute**

PREFACE

This book is an attempt to clarify in simple terms all the dances that are mentioned by name in Shakespeare's plays, as well as other dances that would be appropriate in cases where his text calls for a dance but does not specify one. The dances he mentions are the popular social dances from the fifteenth and sixteenth centuries.

A number of books define these dances beautifully and in great detail, but they are largely works designed for academic purposes and are often difficult for the layperson to understand. It is hoped that the present volume will begin to fill the need for concise information about the nature of each dance and its history, as well as describe its basic steps, thereby assisting actors, directors, and choreographers working on Shakespearean productions involving dances or masques.

The first chapter covers instances in the plays where the only indication given in the text is a stage direction calling for "a dance." The second chapter provides similar coverage for the Shakespearean masque. The next ten chapters are devoted to the individual dances mentioned in the bard's plays either literally as a dance or using a dance as a metaphor.

Directors, of course, may choose to relocate the action of a particular play in a country or historical period other than the bard's. As this practice seems to be increasing in popularity, an appendix to this book lists a large number of dances, modern and ancient, that seem to be appropriate parallels in mood and tempo to the ones of Shakespeare's day. These out-of-period dances will be named and briefly described but not discussed. That is another book.

The illustrations are designed to be as light-hearted and humorous as were social gatherings in Shakespeare's England. It is important to remember that these dances were popular because they were fun to do, and they gave men and women a social contact that was delightfully close. Just as dances do today.

INTRODUCTION

How does a song-and-dance man go from working in musical comedies and nightclub revues to writing a book on the dances mentioned by Shakespeare?

My interest in dancing came very early, by age six or so. My fascination with art in general came even earlier, at about four, when I began to help my mother make patchwork quilts. She was bedridden at the time, and we hung all the colored patches on a clothesline strung between the bedposts. Mom would ask me to pass her squares of blue or red or green as she needed them, thereby teaching me, little by little, the entire spectrum of colors.

She also introduced me to music. From 1923 till her marriage in 1926, Mom led an all-girl orchestra called the McManis Melody Maids. She had been classically trained and was teaching piano at the Strousburg Conservatory of Music in St. Louis, but her orchestra played strictly for social dancing. "Doodle Dee Do" was their theme song. Her marriage led to the demise of the Melody Maids. But music still played a large part in our home. Mom, my brother, and I used to clean house to music. Not only did we sweep, dust, or whatever to tempo, but Mom would designate which part of the musical arrangement we were to clean to. For instance, she would put on a recording. It might be classical or Dixieland or something by one of the big swing bands. I would clean to the percussion. My brother would clean to the brass. My mom would clean to the strings. Then we would switch. Maybe one of us would start doing our chores to the reed section or the piano. If you did not hear your instrument, you stopped work. When you heard it again you resumed. I do not know how clean the house got, but it was a great game for kids. It also did wonders in training my ear to hear and my body to move to music. Years later I developed the housecleaning exercise as a way of teaching acting students to listen and move to music.

I continued studying tap, jazz, and ballet until high school, when I became much more interested in my social life. I continued to dance for school shows and functions but stopped taking classes in dance. My art teacher encouraged and nurtured my interest in the visual arts. I enrolled as a fine arts major at Drury College in Springfield, Missouri. That was a while back; I believe they call it Drury University now.

Then, however, I found that movie musicals were slowly but surely taking over my life. I would see them over and over and practice the dances I saw on the screen on the way home from the cinema. I got a job as an usher at the local movie theater so I would not have to pay to get in. (I saw *Singin' in the Rain* fifty-two times.) I decided I had to pursue a career in show business, so I left college and went back home to St. Louis. Needing to find some kind of a job, I went into training to become a ballroom dance teacher at the Ray Quinlan Dance Studio in St. Louis. That ballroom training has held me in good stead. I am still using it fifty years later.

While working at the dance studio I met Reina, the best-known dancer in the city. The Latin dances were all the rage. Mambo, cha-cha and merengue headed the list. Reina and I became dance partners and developed an act: Jimmy and Reina, Queen of the Mambo. We performed in the Crown Room at the Kingsway Hotel, the Starlight Roof at the Chase Hotel, and taught mambo and cha-cha poolside at the Chase. At this time Mae West and her muscle men were performing at the Chase Club. The muscle men were staying at the Kingsway Hotel where Reina and I were performing. They used to come into the Crown Room after their show for a drink. We got to know them, and one night they told me that a dancer in their show was quitting and would I be interested in auditioning for Miss West. I stammered, "Sure," and that spring, in 1955, with Reina's and my family's blessing, I headed for Ciro's in Hollywood, the last stop on the Mae West tour. When the show closed and another job was not forthcoming, I hitchhiked back to St. Louis and picked up where I left off, with the Crown Room, Reina, and the mambo.

Later that year I was on the verge of being drafted into the military. Some school friends of mine discovered we could enlist for a period of two years instead of serving the normal term of three years. Finding it advantageous to be "regular army" as opposed to draftees, we volunteered and became new recruits.

My tour of duty with the army turned out to be a very exciting time: scary, but exciting nonetheless. Our first three days of processing took place at Ft. Leonard Wood, Missouri. The worst three days of my life. Don't ask. I was then sent to Ft. Riley, Kansas, for basic training. They trained me to be a radio operator. My sergeant told me the life expectancy in combat for a radio operator was three minutes. I did not desert, but I did sneak out of my barracks one night to audition for the Fifth Army Entertainment Division. Hallelujah! They brought me to Fifth Army headquarters in Chicago to dance on a weekly TV army show at WGN-TV. I did two shows a month for three months. These shows were taped and used for army recruitment. Then I entered the All Army Talent Contest. This competition was divided into categories: solo singers, singing groups, solo musicians, musical groups, and specialty performers such as comics, dancers, jugglers, and acrobats. The only performing contest I had entered prior to this was on television in Springfield, Missouri, where I lost to two blind girls singing "Whispering Hope." So, I was not too optimistic about my chances. You had to win at your home base in order to advance to the next level, which was the Fifth Army contest at Camp Carson in Colorado Springs, Colorado. I improvised a dance number to Pee Wee Hunt's "Twelfth Street Rag" and won in my category. That sent me off to Colorado, where I put together a travelogue of dance and won again. That sent me to the All Army Talent Contest at Ft. Dix, New Jersey. I placed third in my category and was rewarded by being assigned to a special show in Quantico, Virginia, for President Eisenhower; the "Ed Sullivan Soldier Show" on CBS in New York City; and, best of all, a world tour in a revue called "Rolling Along of 1956." This all-soldier show entertained our troops stationed throughout the world. We played twenty-seven countries and thirty-eight states in seven months. After the tour I returned to Ft. Riley, where I was assigned to the post library to finish out my tour of duty (no dancin'—but no rifle totin' either).

Scott Jackson, another member of the "Rolling Along" tour, had been the production singer at a supper club in Paris called La Nouvelle Eve before he was drafted. After his discharge, he returned to Paris to resume his career. As I was soon to be discharged, he wired me that they were losing a dancer, and if I was interested I should send some nude photos to the business manager of the La Nouvelle Eve. I figured the French liked nudity with their supper, so I had an army photographer take some scantily clad shots of me and sent them off to Paris. They hired me to replace a Brazilian dancer who was homesick for Rio. So, as soon as I was discharged from the army, I moved to Paris. Wow! Just like Gene Kelly in *An American in Paris*. Not quite. I danced in a posing strap with my body painted silver with a beautiful redheaded French girl who weighed 138 pounds. One night as we were going into a lift, the chiffon from her headdress got caught under my foot. I slipped and dropped her and the La Nouvelle Eve dropped me. Bye bye Paris, bye bye Scott, bye bye beautiful red-haired girl. Hello, St. Louis, the Crown Room, Reina, and the mambo.

Upon my return I found that my cousin, Dave, was a supervisor at the Arthur Murray Dance Studio in St. Louis. He hired me to teach and train new teachers. A few months later he bought an Arthur Murray franchise in Corpus Christi, Texas, and took me along. But I grew weary of teaching ballroom dance and decided I wanted to return to California. Short of funds, I needed to save some money for the move. I landed a job at Coastal States Gas Producing Company. In those days if you could print well, oil company drafting departments could put your talent to use. So I trained and became a geological draftsman. For five years that was my day job. But at night I continued studying dance, worked whenever I could in the local community and performed in musicals at Del Mar College. Jeannine Hager, who headed the theater program there, is the person who set me on the path toward becoming a choreographer. She said, "You have the eye of a painter and the heart of a dancer. When you put those two things together, it spells 'choreography.'" So under the tutelage of Jeannine and Ilsa Elsie, the local dance teacher, I began to develop my craft.

We created a summer stock theater called the Sandy Shores Musical Theatre. The fall of 1963, Emily Jefferson (a pioneer in children's theater), Pat Starr (an actress), Shirley Caballero (a dancer), and I packed up a U-Haul trailer, grabbed up Gypsy the poodle, and headed for New York City. With eighty bucks in my pocket, I arrived in Manhattan, ready to conquer the world of theater.

My first job in New York City was as an artist for Lipman Advertising Agency, a good full-time job. But it was not "showbiz." So I finally gave it up and began doing a variety of part-time jobs while pursuing work in theater. I did not have any of the office skills that the temporary services needed, nor was waiting tables my forte. But I was able to land some interesting jobs like proofreading holes on data-processing cards for Bantam Books, working on Walter Cronkite's staff on the Lyndon Johnson and Barry Goldwater presidential election, freelancing my painting and carpentry skills, and occasionally working as a movie extra. Over the years I had highs and lows, but I stuck to it. The William Morris Talent Agency signed me. I almost got a network variety show and just missed getting a couple of Broadway shows. But it was not to be. I worked off-Broadway, industrials (aka corporate shows), summer stock, revue houses, opera houses, dinner theaters, educational theaters, regional theaters, and theaters abroad.

One of the highs was the Asolo Theatre, a LORT (League Of Regional Theatres) rotating repertory theater in Sarasota, Florida. Howard Millman, the managing director, hired me as choreographer for several productions. Robert Strane and Eberle Thomas, the co-artistic directors, nurtured and challenged me in areas of the theater I knew nothing about. I had to do a great deal of research to produce the quality of stage movement their productions required. A whole new world opened up to me. It was at the Asolo that I first encountered Shakespeare's, *The Two Gentlemen of Verona*, directed by Eberle Thomas. The production was set in the Old West, and it was something very new and fascinating to me. I had choreographed musical comedies based on Shakespeare's plays, such as *West Side Story, Kiss Me Kate,* and *The Boys from Syracuse,* but I had never worked on one of Shakespeare's scripts before.

In another season at the Asolo, while strolling through the rose gardens at the Ringling Museum, Robert Strane handed me a script of *Macbeth* and asked me what I thought of it. I remember telling him, "A long time between numbers, Bob." What did I know? Since that time I have had the good fortune to have designed dances and movement for more than fifteen Shakespearean productions. Some more than once. Creating the dances and movement for one of the bard's plays as well as other classics and period pieces became one of the most exciting ways for me to express myself artistically, and it still is. However, outside of the witches, *Macbeth* still has a long time between numbers.

When Florida State University moved their graduate acting program to the Asolo Theatre and developed the FSU/Asolo Conservatory, Dean Richard Fallon asked me to be the movement and dance teacher. Marty

Ingle headed the conservatory and taught acting. Mary Corrigan taught voice. Marty and Mary moved on to positions elsewhere and were replaced by Neal Kenyon and Ruby Allen, respectively. John France-schina taught music and singing. I taught dance and period movement. I was also the staff choreographer for the Asolo Theatre. A happy quartet were we.

Eight years later I took an offer from Penn State University. Working with fine educators and directors like Helen Manfull, Lowell Manfull, Bill Kelly, Barry Kur, Michael Connally, and Bob Leonard aided in my growth as an artist. While teaching there I began to receive calls from various directors and choreographers around the country asking how to execute specific dances mentioned in Shakespeare's text and stage directions. Hence, the idea for this book.

In 1996, I returned to the Asolo Theatre and the FSU/Asolo Conservatory. Here I continue to choreograph, teach workshops, and do research on period dances and movement. This book comes from twenty years of procrastination and a year of good hard work. I am very grateful to a great many people who helped me turn a lot of corners to find my way from shaking my hips with Reina, Queen of the Mambo, to writing a book about how Shakespeare kicked up his heels.

LIST OF ILLUSTRATIONS

List of Musical Examples

ACKNOWLEDGMENTS

I am thankful and grateful to:

Jeannine Hager for introducing me to the world of choreography.

Emily Jefferson for teaching me more about appreciating art, literature, and the theater than she will ever know. And for her love and encouragement since our friendship began.

Richard Fallon for his faith in my ability to teach.

Robert Strane for introducing me to the world of Shakespeare and for constantly challenging me to excel.

Eberle Thomas for his support and advice in writing this book and his use of my choreography in numerous productions under his direction.

Howard Millman for his loyalty and trust in my abilities and bringing me to the Asolo Theatre.

Lowell Manfull and *Helen Manfull* for their enormous support, care, and love, and my gratitude to Helen for her invaluable help and sound advice in the writing of this book.

Michael Sebastian for his help and advice in the selection of music.

Kate Holgate for her aid in researching and gathering the dances in Shakespeare's text. And for her care and encouragement on this project.

Carl Meyer for his support, encouragement, and love.

Karin Baker, Greg Kayne, Neal Kenyon, Scott Jackson, Gil Lazier, Dan Carter, Stephan DeGhelder, and *Don Creason* for the love, support, wisdom, and good advice they have shared with me throughout my career.

And to the dancers, singers, actors, musicians, designers, choreographers, directors, producers, teachers, and students with whom I have worked, studied, and taught over the past fifty years.

ABOUT THE AUTHOR

Jim Hoskins (Society of Stage Directors and Choreographers) started studying tap dance at the age of six in St. Louis, Missouri. Jazz, modern, and ballet were to follow. He attended Brentwood High School in St. Louis and then Drury College in Springfield, Missouri, where he majored in fine art. His multifaceted career has taken him from Ciro's in Hollywood, to La Nouvelle Eve in Paris, to the Upstairs at the Downstairs in New York City. Mr. Hoskins began his professional career in a Latin dance act with partner Reina, Queen of the  Mambo and has since performed, directed, and choreographed in educational theater, television, film, the corporate theater, opera, nightclubs, and legitimate and musical theater. He has staged over 400 productions in the United States and abroad. Over the past thirty years Mr. Hoskins has taught period style, movement, and dance. He taught in both the graduate and undergraduate programs at Penn State University and the graduate program in acting at Florida State University. Mr. Hoskins resides in Sarasota, Florida, where he is an adjunct professor of theatre at the FSU/Asolo Conservatory and staff choreographer for the Asolo Theatre.

Figure 1.1   Reverence (Bow)

CHAPTER 1
STAGE DIRECTION (DANCE)

In Shakespeare's stage directions there is no mention of specific dances to be used. The dances that I have suggested are ones he mentions in the text throughout his plays. There are other dances that were popular during his time: the allemande, a German round dance used in square dancing today; the bourree, a French clog dance performed in pairs, with the dancers using a skipping step to dance around one another; and the saraband from Spain, a sexual pantomime that was considered so indecent it was banned in public until the French court tamed it for acceptance. And then there is the trecone from Italy. Four couples would perform this dance in a square or circle to honor a particular event, such as civic celebration or a marriage. The trecone is danced in 2/4 time. The others mentioned above are in 3/4 time. Or a choreographer or director might want to create a dance of his/her own that enhances the production.

THE LIFE OF KING HENRY VIII

Act I, scene iv

    CARDINAL WOLSEY: Say, lord chamberlain,
They have done my poor house grace; for which I pay'em A thousand
thanks, and pray'em take their pleasures.
    [They choose ladies for the DANCE. King Henry chooses Anne.]

    KING HENRY: The fairest hand I ever touched: O beauty, Till now I
never knew thee!
    [Music. DANCE.]

A measure, pavan (Chapter 10), or branle (Chapter 4) could be used here.
However, if the music chosen is a faster tempo, a coronto (Chapter 6) is
also appropriate.

MACBETH

Act IV, scene i

    I. WITCH: I'll charm the air to give a sound
While you perform your antic round,
That this great king will kindly say
Our duties did his welcome pay.
    [Music. The Witches DANCE, and vanish.]

The witches can dance individually and/or perform a type of roundel
(Chapter 12). The witches' sabbath is a time at night when witches and
demons meet to concoct mischief. This meeting concludes with a dance in
which they all turn their backs to each other. While the meaning of this
action is unknown, it can be useful in choreographing the witches' dances.

A MIDSUMMER NIGHT'S DREAM

Act V, scene i

    TITANIA: First rehearse your song by rote,
To each word a warbling note.
Hand in hand, with fairy grace,
will we sing, and bless this place.
    [Song and DANCE]

A roundel (Chapter 12), a measure (Chapter 10), or a branle (Chapter 4) are all possible choices for this scene. The tempo can vary greatly in these dances, giving the choreographer considerable freedom in his or her design.

PERICLES, PRINCE OF TYRE

Act II, scene iii

> KING: I not have excuse with saying this:
> Loud music is too harsh for ladies' heads,
> Since they love men in the arms as well as beds.
> [The Knights DANCE]
> So, this was well asked, 'twas so well performed.
> Come, sir.
> Here is a lady that wants breathing too;
> And I have heard, you knights of Tyre
> Are excellent in making ladies trip,
> And that their measures are as excellent.
>
> PERICLES: In those that practice them they are, my lord.
>
> KING: O, that's as much as you would be denied
> Of your fair courtesy.
> [The Knights and Ladies DANCE]

The knights' dance could be a morris dance (Chapter 11) or a morris with use of swords. They also danced a pantomime telling the story of a battle won with great sacrifice. Mock battles were stereotyped parts of many entertainments of the period. The dance was called the pyrrhic, a warrior dance dating back to the ancient Greeks.

Thoinot Arbeau, the sixteenth-century dancing master, writes of the Maltese Branle danced by the Knights of Malta. The men and women dance a circular branle, then rush to the center of the circle and back again. They continue the circular branle. This is the type of movement that could be used for the knights and their ladies. Check the chapters on the branle and the measure (Chapters 4 and 10).

ROMEO AND JULIET

Act I, scene v

CAPULET: Welcome, gentlemen! Ladies that have their toes
Unplagued with corns will walk about with you.
Ah ha, my mistresses! Which of you all
Will now deny to dance? She that makes dainty,
She I'll swear hath corns. Am I come near ye now?
Welcome, gentlemen! I have seen the day
That I have worn a visor and could tell
A whispering tale in a fair lady's ear,
Such as would please. 'Tis gone, 'tis gone, 'tis gone!
You are welcome, gentlemen! Come, musicians, play.
[Music plays and they DANCE.]

Several dances could be used in this scene. A measure or pavan (Chapter 10), the morris dance (Chapter 11), the canary (Chapter 5), or the coranto (Chapter 6), or even the galliard and la volta (Chapters 7 and 9).

THE LIFE OF TIMON OF ATHENS

Act I, scene ii

[The Lords rise from table, with much adoring of Timon, and to show their loves, each single out an Amazon, and all DANCE, men with women, a lofty strain or two to the hautboys, and cease]

This calls for a bigger than life, strutting kind of promenade, as in a pavan (Chapter 10), a lively branle (Chapter 4), a tordion (Chapter 7), or a canary (Chapter 5).

THE TEMPEST

Act III, scene iii

SEBASTIAN: [aside to Antonio] I say to-night. No more.
[Solemn and strange music; Prospero on the top (invisible). Enter several strange Shapes, bringing in a banquet; and DANCE about it with gentle actions of salutations; and, inviting the King & c. To eat, they depart]

An individual movement, dance, and pantomime are used to set the scene, as in the beginning of a masque (Chapter 2).

Act III, scene iii

ARIEL: Thee of thy son, Alonso,
They have bereft; and do pronounce by me
Ling'ring perdition (worse than any death
Can be at once) shall step by step attend
You and your ways; whose wraths to guard you from,
Which here, in this most desolate isle, else falls
Upon your heads, is nothing but hearts sorrow
And a clear life ensuing.
[He vanishes in thunder; then, to soft music, enter the Shapes again, and DANCE with mocks and mows, and carrying out the table.]

A dance and pantomime are designed to change the scene. Chapter 2, on masques, could be helpful.

Act IV, scene i

IRIS: You nymphs, called Naiades, of the windring brooks
With sedged crowns and ever-harmful looks,
Leave your crisp channels, and on this green land
Answer your summons; Juno does command.
Come, temperate nymphs, and help to celebrate
A contract of true love: be not too late.
[Enter certain Nymphs]
You sunburned sicklemen, of August weary,
Come hither from the furrow and be merry.
Make holiday: your rye-straw hats put on,
And these fresh nymphs encounter every one
In country footing.
[Enter certain Reapers, properly habited. They join with the Nymphs in a graceful DANCE; toward the end where of Prospero starts suddenly and speaks; after which, to a strange, hollow, and confused noise, they heavenly vanish.]

See the steps and combinations used in the branle/hay (Chapter 4), the coranto (Chapter 6), and the measure (Chapter 10).

THE WINTER'S TALE

Act IV, scene iv

CLOWN: Not a word, a word! We stand upon our manners.
Come, strike up!
[Music. Here a DANCE OF SHEPHERDS AND SHEPHERD-
ESSES.]

POLIXENES: Pray, good sheperd, what fair swain is this
Which dances with your daughter?

SHEPHERD: They call him Doricles, and boasts himself
To have a worthy feeding. But I have it
Upon his own report and I believe it;
He looks like sooth. He says he loves my daughter.
I think so too, for never gazed the moon
Upon the water as he'll stand and read
As 'twere my daughter's eyes; and, to be plain,
I think that there is not half a kiss to choose
Who loves another best.

POLIXENES: She dances featly.

Lincoln Kirstein's *Book of the Dance* mentions an English country dance
known as Sheperds Hey. Arbeau calls it Branle de la Haye. This is the hay
discussed in Chapter 4.

Act IV, scene iv

SERVANT: Master, there is three carters, three shepherds, three
neatherds, three swineherds, that they have made themselves all men of
hair. They call themselves Saltiers, and they have a dance which the
wenches say is a gallimaufry of gambols, because they are not in't; but they
themselves are o' th' mind, if it be not too rough for some that know little
but bowling, it will please plentifully.

SHEPHERD: Away! We'll none on't. Here has been too much homely
foolery already. I know, sir we weary you.

POLIXENES: You weary those that refresh us. Pray, let's see these
four threes of herdsmen.

SERVANT: One three of them, by their own report, sir, hath danced before the king; and not the worst of the three but jumps twelve foot and a half by th' squire.

SHEPHERD: Leave your prating. Since these good men are pleased, let them come in; but quickly now.

SERVANT: Why, they stay at door, sir. [Exit]
[Here a DANCE OF TWELVE SATYRS.]

The satyr plays of the ancient Greek theatre featured a lewd dance called the Sikinnis (Figure 1.2). The dancers wore pink costumes with attachable horsehair tails and phalloi. It was a lively, vigorous dance with hunched bodies and a trotting, syncopated beat. The dance was ill-tempered, brutish, and violent. It had acrobatics with leaps, jumps, turns, kicks, and stamping feet accompanied by whoops and shouts. The satyr dance had both gravity and gaiety. It was performed in a grotesquely comic manner, but had the form of tragedy. It was like a macabre clown.

Figure 1.2   The Dance of Twelve Satyrs

It is argued that the dance of the twelve satyrs is imitated from Ben Jonson's Masque of Oberon, performed at court on January 1, 1611. *A Winter's Tale* played at the Globe sometime between that date and May 15, 1611. Ben Jonson's actual text of this masque can be found in *The Works of Ben Jonson,* edited by William Gifford (1853). This is the scenario of that masque.

The scene: a large dark rock with trees behind it. The moon is just beginning to show. A satyr is seen by moonlight. He comes forth and calls to the other satyrs but none appear. He calls again and thinks he is answered, but it is only an echo. Again he calls, and a second satyr answers and then appears. Ten more appear from all over the set, leaping and performing ludicrous acts and gestures. Among them is Silene, the most famous of the satyrs. He and the other satyrs speak in prose, praising Oberon, the fairy prince. They will dance and pay him homage with their antics. Then the scene opens to show a transparent palace. Two armed Sylvans (spirits of the forest) guard the palace gates. Both are sound asleep. Silene and the other satyrs discuss many mischievous ways in which to awaken the Sylvans: strip them, whip them, put a wasp in their nostrils, an eel in their guts, or just hit them over the head with their clubs. They decide to tickle them awake. The Sylvans slowly awaken, giggling. Silene upbraids them for being asleep at their post. The Sylvans tell the satyrs that they are too early and to go away and dance until the cock crows and the gates open. The satyrs sing a song and dance a brawl. They go into a wild dance full of gestures and swift motion, whereupon the cock crows.

In the next scene the gates open and all the satyrs stop their dances and bow their heads. The Fairy Nation is discovered. They are playing musical instruments, singing, and dancing. Knights and masquers sit about. There is a large fanfare announcing Oberon. He is in a chariot drawn by two white bears and guarded by three Sylvans, one on each side and one leading the procession. A song brings the chariot forth as the satyrs go into another joyful and frolicsome dance. The lead Sylvan quiets the fracas to exalt the majesty of Oberon. Silene steps forth and does the same. The elves and fairies come forward. Two of the fairies sing a song. After the song the other fairies perform a dance, which is followed by another song praising Oberon. The knights and Oberon step forward and dance. This is followed by still another song and a second dance by Oberon and his knights. Then the fairies sing another song, followed by the entire company dancing the measures, corantos, and galliards until Phosphorus, the daystar, appears to call them away. One of the Sylvans sings a song here. Phosphorus again calls them to rest. After this they all dance the last dance, sing their last song, and exit as the gate closes and the masque, at last, comes to an end.

Figure 2.1 Masques

CHAPTER 2
MASQUES

THE THIRD PART OF KING HENRY VI

Act III, scene iii

    LEWIS: Then, England's messenger, return in post
    And tell false Edward, thy supposed king,
    That Lewis of France is sending over MASQUERS[1]
    To revel it with him and his new bride.
    Thou seest what's passed. Go fear thy king withal.

In Act IV, scene i, a post quotes Lewis' above message to King Edward.

---

[1]Masquers: Participants in a courtly dramatic performance or revel (ironically). R.K. Turner, Jr. and G.W. Williams, eds. *The Second and Third Parts of King Henry the Sixth*. In A. Harbage, ed., *The Complete Pelican Shakespeare*. Baltimore: Penguin Books, 1969.

THE LIFE OF KING HENRY VIII

Act I, scene i

NORFOLK: Then you lost
The view of earthly glory. Men might say
Till this time pomp was single, but now married
To one above itself. Each following day
Became the next day's master, till the last
Made former wonders, its. To-day the French,
All clinquant, all in gold, like the heathen gods
Shone down the English; and to-morrow they
Made Britain India—every man that stood
Showed like a mine. Their dwarfish pages were
As cherubins, all gilt. The madams too,
Not used to toil, did almost sweat to bear
The pride upon them, That their very labor
Was to them as a painting. Now this MASQUE
Was cried incomparable; and th' ensuing night
Made it a fool and beggar. The two kings,
Equal in lustre, were now best, now worst,
As presence did present them: him in eye
Still him in praise; and being present both,
'Twas said they saw but one, and no discerner
Durst wag his tongue in censure. When these suns
(For so they phrase 'em) by their heralds challenge
The noble spirits to arms, they did perform
Beyond thought's compass, that former fabulous story,
Being now seen possible enough, got credit,
That Bevis was believed.

THE LIFE AND DEATH OF KING JOHN

Act V, scene ii

PHILIP THE BASTARD: By all the blood that ever fury breathed,
The youth says well. Now hear our English king,
For thus his royalty doth speak in me.
He is prepared, and reason too he should.
This apish and unmannerly approach,
This harnessed MASQUE and undivised revel,
This unhaired sauciness and boyish troops,
The king doth smile at, and is well prepared
To whip this dwarfish war, these pigmy arms,
From out the circles of his territories.

THE MERCHANT OF VENICE

Act II, scene iv

LORENZO: Go, gentlemen;
Will you prepare you for this MASQUE to-night?
I am provided of a torchbearer.

Act II, scene v

LAUNCELOT (Clown): And they have conspired together. I will not say you will see a MASQUE, but if you do, then it was not for nothing that my nose fell a-bleeding on Black Monday last at six o'clock i' th' morning, falling out of that year on Ash Wednesday was four year in th' afternoon.

SHYLOCK: What, are there MASQUES? Hear you me, Jessica:
Lock up my doors; and when you hear the drum
And the vile squealing of the wry-necked fife,
Clamber not you up to the casements then,
Nor thrust your head into the public street
To gaze on Christian fools with varnished faces;
But stop my house's ears—I mean my casements;
Let not the sound of shallow fopp'ry enter
My sober house. By Jacob's staff I swear
I have no mind of feasting forth to-night;

But I will go. Go you before me, sirrah.
Say I will come.

A MIDSUMMER NIGHT'S DREAM

Act V, scene i

THESEUS: Come now, what MASQUES[2] what dances shall we have,
To wear away this long age of three hours
Between our after-supper and bedtime?
Where is our usual manager of mirth?
What revels are in hand? Is there no play
To ease the anguish of a torturing hour?
Call Philostrate.

PHILOSTRATE: Here, mighty Theseus.

THESEUS: Say, what abridgement have you for this evening?
What MASQUE? What music? How shall we beguile
The lazy time, if not with some delight?

THE LIFE OF TIMON OF ATHENS

Act I, scene ii

TIMON: They're welcome all; let 'em have kind admittance.
Music, make their welcome!

I. LORD: You see, my lord, how ample y' are beloved.
[Music. Enter Cupid, with the MASQUE of Ladies
as Amazons with lutes in their hands, dancing
and playing.]

APEMANTUS: Hoy-day!
What a sweep of vanity comes this way!
They dance? They are mad women.
Like madness is the glory of this life
As this pomp shows to a little oil and root.
We make ourselves fools to disport ourselves

---

[2]Masques: Courtly shows featuring a dance of masked figures. M. Doran, ed. *A Midsummer Night's Dream*. In A. Harbage, ed., *The Complete Pelican Shakespeare*. Baltimore: Penguin Books, 1969.

And spend our flatteries to drink those men
Upon whose age we void it up again
With poisonous spite and envy.
Who lives that's not depraved or depraves?
Who dies that spares but not one spurn to their graves
Of their friends' gift?
I should fear those that dance before me now
Would one day stamp upon me. 'T has been done.
Men shut their doors against a setting sun.
[The Lords rise from table, with much adoring of Timon, and to show
their loves, each single out an Amazon, and all dance, men with women, a
lofty strain or two to the hautboys, and cease.]

TIMON: You have done our pleasures much grace, fair ladies,
Set a fair fashion on our entertainment,
Which was not half so beautiful and kind;
You have added worth unto't and lustre,
And entertained me with mine own device.[3]
I am to thank you for 't.

Twelfth Night, or What You Will

Act I, scene iii

SIR ANDREW: I'll stay a month longer. I am a fellow o' th' strangest
mind i' th' world. I delight in MASQUES and revels sometimes all
together.

The masque was an established institution long before Shakespeare's time.
*Love's Labour's Lost, A Midsummer Night's Dream, Much Ado About Noth-
ing,* for example, all have features from the masque.

The English court masques first made their appearance early in the
reign of King Henry VIII and continued until the success of the Puritan
Revolution. They were founded on masquerade parties that included plays
and dancing from medieval times and featured mummings (players in
masks).

---

[3]Apparently Timon himself composed the masque. C. Hinman, ed. *The Life of Timon of Athens.* In
A. Harbage, ed., *The Complete Pelican Shakespeare.* Baltimore: Penguin Books, 1969.

Figure 2.2   A Renaissance Band

Often a stage with scenery was wheeled into the Great Hall. On the stage in front of the scenery was a group of performers. All of this was accompanied by music. At a suitable time, the performers would come down from their stage and dance a prepared ballet. They sometimes took partners from the audience for social dancing, called commoning or communing, as in Shakespeare's *Henry VIII* (Act I, scene iv). The king comes to Wolsey's feast with a party of mummers and afterward dances with Anne Boleyn. It was not unusual for royalty to perform masques.

These entertainments followed a set formula. There was a theme to connect the various "entries," or acts or parts. The gods and goddesses, the muses, and legends such as Robin Hood and Maid Marian (as mentioned in the chapter on morris dancing) are examples of some of the ideas used. The first entry would be of the noble performers in glorious costumes, then songs and speeches, followed by a dance. After this, the performers would exit to change costumes. A grotesque interlude acted by professional comics would then be performed. This was called the anti-masque, a comic interlude that parodied the major plot. The comics would perform morris dances, sword dances, galliards, jigs, and corantos. Then a second entry for the courtiers came next. The number of entries varied, but they were always separated by the anti-masques. Masques hit their

their peak in the seventeenth century under the guidance of playwright Ben Jonson and designer and architect Inigo Jones. They emphasized dialogue and song, giving the masque a substantial literary framework along with the lavish, ornate, and elaborate spectacle for which they were known. Jonson and Jones ushered in the golden age of the masque during the reign of James I and his pleasure-loving wife, Anne. To quote William Rose Benet in *The Reader's Encyclopedia*, "These masques had a lyrical grace and a sumptuous splendor that has never been equalled in stage entertainments." I'm sure many showmen since that day would argue that point.

In Lincoln Kirstein's *The Book of the Dance, A Short History of Classic Theatrical Dancing* (1942) there is a chapter on the English court masque. The history, structure, and scenarios of various masques are explained in great detail. This book, originally published in 1935 under the title of *Dance*, is a treasure.

a

b

Figure 3.1   Bergomask a) Part I b) Part II

CHAPTER 3
BERGOMASK

A MIDSUMMER NIGHT'S DREAM

Act V, scene I

BOTTOM: Will it please you to see the epilogue, or to hear a BER-GOMASK dance between two of our company?

THESEUS: No epilogue, I pray you; for your play needs no excuse. But come, your BERGOMASK: let your epilogue alone. [A dance]

The bergomask (bergamasca) is a fine, raucous, jovial, rustic, country dance that hails from Bergamo, Italy, located northwest of Milano. As every social dance started as a wooing dance, this was probably no exception. The peasants—men and women—join hands and form a large circle. The music is struck up in 2/4 time. The dancers step to every beat of the music as they circle counterclockwise (or clockwise if you wish). After so many measures of music, say eight or sixteen, the music changes tempo or melody. Then the dancers break apart and perform high jumps in the air, crossing their feet front and back as many times as they can before landing. In a more disciplined form (the classic ballet), the jump became known as an entrechat. The dancers would also click their heels together in the air on either side. In musical theater terminology, these leaps are called bells. On the next musical change, the dancers join hands again and continue the circle forward, or go back the opposite way. When the music changes again, the circle breaks and the dancers become couples taking each other by the shoulders or waist and turning around in place. They start the circle again only to break it and possibly change partners. As you can see, there were many variations with which to play. The dance was undisciplined and very boisterous—a true celebration. However, it did not make the transition from the countryside to the royal court. But then neither did the peasants.

BERGOMASK

Musical Example 3.1 Bergomask

Figure 4.1   Brawl/Branle/Hay

CHAPTER 4
BRAWL (BRANLE/HAY)

Act III, scene i

MOTH: Master, will you win your love with a French BRAWL?

ARMADO: How meanest thou? Brawling in French?

MOTH: No, my complete master; but to jig off a tune at the tongue's end, canary to it with your feet, humor it with turning up your eyelids, sigh a note and sing a note, . . . with your hat penthouse-like o'er the shop of your eyes; with your arms crossed on your slim-belly doublet like a rabbit on a spit; or your hands in your pocket like a man after the old painting; and keep not too long in one tune, but a snip and away.

Act V, scene i

DULL: I'll make one in a dance, or so; or I will play on the tabour to the Worthies, and let them dance the HAY.

In several instances, Shakespeare uses the word "brawl" just as we do, to mean noisy, clamorous, and rowdy. In short, a word for roughhouse. He also refers to a dance called the brawl. But the dance was grand and stately as well as rowdy and boisterous. It was originally a French dance called "branle" (pronounced "brawl"). Shakespeare spelled it the way it sounded. The name comes from the French word, "branler," which means to sway;

BRAWL
BRANLE SIMPLE

Musical Example 4.1   Brawl/Branle Simple

a line of dancers swaying first to the left and then to the right. It was the first dance to require instrumental music as accompaniment and was also the first dance to have alternating rhythms, the "quick" and "slow," which are still spoken of by ballroom dance instructors today. "Quick" equals one beat of music, and "slow" equals two beats. There are many variations of brawls. The dance is made up of simples (single step to the side) and doubles (two steps to the side). The dancers clasp hands and make a circle facing into the center. The basic step consists of a double to the left and a simple to the right. Example: Take two side steps (double) on your toes to the left and pause with feet together and a slight bend of the knees (step together, step, pause), then one side step (simple) to the right, and pause with feet together and a slight bend of the knees (step together, pause).

By count (beat) starting on the left foot:

1st beat: side step to the left (L)
2nd beat: bring the right (R) foot to the left, change weight to R
3rd beat: side step to L
4th beat: pause with feet together
5th beat: one side step to R on the R foot 6th beat: bring feet together,
    do not change weight

Repeat the sequence over and over, always starting to the left. Lean your body slightly in the direction you are going: left then right, left then right. The music is in 2/4, 4/4, or 3/4 time. It can be very slow and stately or very quick and lively. The variations in the dance come with the number of steps taken left or right and the tempo and manner in which the steps are executed. For example, in the Branle Gai, the dance is done by taking leaps from side to side as well as kicking at the end of a phrase. The gents may give it a good strong kick. The ladies just lift their foot in the air. To the left side: leap, step, step, kick. Repeat to the right side (count: 1, 2, 3, kick, etc.). In contrast, Thoinot Arbeau, the French dancing master, describes the Branle de l'Official thus: "It begins with a double to the left and a double to the right, repeated. The dancers then proceed continuously to the left during six singles. Then the men take the women by the waist and make them jump and bound into the air." To do the brawl in 3/4 time: two steps to the left 1 (L), 2 (R), 3 (L). Do not bring the right foot to the left, but take it back to the right on 1. Bring the left foot to the right on 2, and settle feet together on 3. It is like a waltz step to the left and a balance to the right.

Besides the two mentioned above, there are other specific branles, such as Branles Coupes, Branle de la Guerre, and the Scots Branle. They have steps designed in sequence. But for your own production, a new branle could be designed if needed. Remember these were all social dances in Shakespeare's day. The dance should be choreographed to fit the needs of the production. Style and manner need to be true to the period but not necessarily the step sequence.

The hay (haye/hey) is a fifteenth-century dance descending from a medieval dance called the Farandole. It is a line dance of holding hands and skipping around in a serpentine manner following the leader. The hay is danced in double time like the coranto or like the dance from the 1960s

BRANLE GAI

Set by Arnold Dolmetsch
M.M. ♩· = 66

Orchesographie

Musical Example 4.2   Branle Gay

THE HAY PASSAGE

Set for keyboard by
Michael Sebastian

Musical Example 4.3   The Hay Passage

called the pony. The dancers would form a long line and drop hands. The line can be of any shape—curved into an S or a circle—or it can break apart and make two lines facing each other as in a reel. The dancers then dance in place, shifting weight from one side to the other or turning on themselves while the dancer on the end rapidly weaves through the stationary dancers. When the first dancer reaches the end of the line, the next dancer follows suit until everyone makes the weave to the opposite end; then they weave back to their original positions. You can also have a constantly moving line. Person #1 changes with person #2, person #2 changes with person #3, person #3 changes with person #4, and so on down the line. The weave is called "making the hay." The hay lives on in the reels and folk dancing and is still as much fun today as it was in Shakespeare's day.

Figure 5.1 Canary

CHAPTER 5
CANARY

ALL'S WELL THAT ENDS WELL

Act II, scene i

   LAFEW: I have seen medicine that's able to breath life into a stone, quicken a rock, and make you dance CANARY[1] with sprightly fire and motion.

LOVE'S LABOUR'S LOST

Act III, scene i

   MOTH: Master, will you win your love with a French brawl?

   ARMADO: How meanest thou? Brawling in French?

   MOTH: No, my complete master; but to jig off a tune at the tongue's end, CANARY to it with your feet.

The canary is a fifteenth-century couples dance from the Spanish Canary Islands. It was originally danced around a corpse or pyre but eventually became a dance celebrating love instead of death, in which the dancers

---

[1] Canary *v.* -ed/-ing/-es: to dance nimbly (as in the CANARY dance). *Webster's Third New International Dictionary.*

began to pantomime innuendos of lovemaking. The source of this change is unknown. However, the canary became a very lively dance, and, as we know, dancing about love can be much more rewarding than dancing about death.

After the initial promenade (a walk around the hall), the gentleman leaves his partner and dances away from and then toward her, using skipping and stamping movements alternately on heel and toe. (Hop, heel, hop, toe. The hop is on one foot while the heel-toe is executed on the other, much like a jig.) The lady then performs before her partner, turning and stomping. The dance in this form was considered so difficult that only the most practiced dancers attempted it. As a result, it had disappeared from the European court by the end of the sixteenth century.

The canary must have displayed great energy and agility in Shakespeare's day. Mabel Dolmetsch, an authority on the court and popular dances of fifteenth- and sixteenth-century Europe, says the peculiarities of the canary are the heel-and-toe step (explained above), the stamp, and the swishing slide (moving to each side in a zig-zag fashion). The canary may have derived from a masquerade or ballet representing savages or Moors. Some say it represented Indians from Peru, North America, or the Canary Islands. The music is in 3/8 or 6/8 time. The rhythm has much more of a light lilt than the driving jig. It is often found in the ballets of Jean Baptiste Lully and Jean Phillipe Rambeau. Francois Couperin and Henry Purcell have also written canaries.

The canary was definitely a spectacular dance. In his *Orchesography*, Thoinot Arbeau states, (1589)

> Some say that this dance comes from the Canary Islands and that it is regularly practiced there. Others, whose opinion I should prefer to share, hold that it is derived from a ballet composed for a masquerade in which the dancers were dressed as Kings and Queens of Mauretania, or rather, like savages, with plumes dyed in various colors. This is the manner of dancing the CANARY. A young man takes a damsel and dancing with her to the phrases of a suitable air, conducts her to the end of the room. This done, he returns to the place where he began, gazing at the damsel the while. He then goes towards her again, making certain passages (steps), and, this done, he returns as before. Then the damsel comes and goes the same in front of him, and afterwards returns

to the place where she was; and both continue these comings and goings as many times as the diversity of passages affords them the means. And note that these passages are lively, yet strange and fantastic, resembling in large measure the dances of savages (Kirstein, p. 160).

There are many variations of the canary. Some have been documented by Thoinot Arbeau in 1587, Cesare Negri in 1604, and Fabritio Caroso in 1581. These appear as specific dances in Mabel Dolmetsch's book, *Dances of Spain and Italy from 1400 to 1600*. The patterns and steps are explained in detail. The following is an example of one of these dances arranged by Cesare Negri for two dancers. Facing front, the dance opens with the medium reverence: Women bend their knees and bow their heads, men step back on their left foot and bend both knees and bow their head. This is followed by two continenzas (side steps left and right). The dancers step to the left, bringing the right foot to the left, raising up on the toes, then settling both feet together and slightly bending the knees. This is repeated to the right. This is executed in four beats to the left and four beats to the right. The partners stand side by side. Starting on the left foot they advance toward center, hand in hand, with four sliding broken sequences (on left foot slide-hop, on right foot slide-hop, on left foot slide-hop, on right foot slide-hop). It is like ice-skating without skates. The partners drop hands and link right arms, revolving toward the right with four more slide-hop steps. They drop arms and link left arms, revolving to the left in the same manner. Releasing their hold, they break apart, make a short bow, and go to opposite ends of the stage. The lady veers to her left and faces upstage, and the man goes to his right and faces downstage, obliquely facing each other about eight feet apart. They then dance the four slide-hop steps toward each other in an S shape—the lady curving upstage, downstage, and upstage, the man curving downstage, upstage, and downstage, whereupon they do a quarter turn on the right toe and do a cadenza (a little jump) to face each other. The grand reverence (a bow that takes twice as long in tempo as the medium reverence) ends the dance. The music is in 2/2 and counted 1-2, 1-2. Slide on 1, hop on 2. An optional way to start the step is to syncopate the first beat by hopping into the slide step (count: 5, 6, 7, 8, *and* 1). Hop on an "and" count so that the first step is still on the first count of the measure. (count: *and* 1, 2). Hop on the right foot ("and") then slide onto the left foot (Count 1). Repeat on

Continenzas: Tempo in 2/2 Time	Count	Step
Measure/bar one	1	L side
	2	R (together)
Measure/bar two	1	Raise up on toes
	2	Settle with knees bent
Measure/bar three	1	R side
	2	L (together)
Measure/bar four	1	Raise up on toes
	2	Settle with knees bent

To syncopate add an "and" count to the first beat.

Sliding Broken Sequences	Count	Step
Measure/bar one	1	L forward
	2	L hop
Measure/bar two	1	R forward
	2	R hop

Repeat steps on measures 3 and 4.

Heel and Toe	Count	Step
Measure/bar one	&	Hop on left foot
	1	Point right toe and cross left ankle
	&	Hop on left foot
	2	Put right heel on floor with flexed foot and straight leg

If repeated on the other side, it is very much like a jig.

the right side. Hop-slide-hop, hop-slide-hop, and so on. It would start the same way the polka is begun.

This is very basic but gives you a brief idea of how the canary is danced. With accomplished dancers it could be known as a challenge dance. Each dancer trying to outdo the other in an improvisational manner: turning, lunging, jumping, hopping heel-toeing and stamping like a flamenco dancer. Just don't forget the dyed plumes Arbeau describes. It couldn't hurt.

CANARY
II. Canario (Cesare Negri)

Musical Example 5.1   Canary: II. Canario (Cesare Negri)

Figure 6.1 Coranto

CHAPTER 6
CORANTO/COURANTE

ALL'S WELL THAT ENDS WELL

Act II, scene iii

LAFEW: Lustick! as the Dutchman says. I'll like a maid the better whilst I have a tooth in my head. Why, he's able to lead her a CORANTO[1].

THE LIFE OF KING HENRY V

Act III, scene v

DUKE OF BOURBON: They bid us to the English dancing schools
And teach lavoltas high, and swift CORANTOS,
Saying our grace is only in our heels
And that we are most lofty runaways.

---

[1] COURANT also COURANTO (küränt, -ant) *n*. -s [MF courante, fr. Fem of courant, pres. part. OF courir to run]: 1. A dance of Italian origin marked by quick running steps. B; A similar but graver and more formal dance developed in France in the seventeenth century. 2. Music for a courante or having the rhythm of a courante that is a rather quick 3/2 measure and is characterized by dotted notes and shifts to 6/4 measure. 3. Dial. Eng. A running about: romp, carouse. *Webster's Third New International Dictionary.*

Twelfth Night, or, What You Will

Act I, scene iii

SIR TOBY BELCH: Wherefore are these things hid? Wherefore have these gifts a curtain before 'em? Are they like to take a dust, like Mistress Mall's picture? Why dost thou not go to church in a galliard and come home in a CORANTO?

The coranto was one of the most popular court dances of the sixteenth century. In Elizabethan times it was a lively skipping dance in triple time. The dance begins with the usual bow (reverence). The couples hold hands (women on the right) and dance clockwise in a large circle. The basic step is with the partners on the left foot, skipping to the left side. It may be described as follows: step together, step/or step ball, change/or like the soft-shoe step in tap dancing/or chasse. The dancers repeat the skip on the right foot, take two long running steps or leaps (jeté) forward, and skip on the left side again.

There are many differences of opinion as to how the coranto should be danced. The music can change from 3/4 time to 6/4 to 3/2. Arbeau quotes four bars of music for a coranto in 2/2 time. Choreographer and author Bari Rolfe counts it in 2/4 time as shown above. Dancers may dance around the room, around in a small circle, around each other, forward and back, or a combination of all the above. Many patterns can be introduced. It can be great fun, a bit of a romp, and exhausting. In Elizabeth's court they liked to kick up a ruckus with their dancing now and again.

The first form of the coranto was one of the dances brought over from Italy to France by Catherine de Medici. The second form had its origin in France and is the true court form to which the coranto owes its long and great popularity (about 1550 to 1750). Originally, there seems to have been a pantomime dance or a prelude to the actual dance. As Arbeau in his *Orchesography* explains,

> In my young days there was a kind of game and ballet arranged to the Courante. For three young men would choose three girls, and having placed themselves in a row, the first dancer would lead his damsel to the end of the room, when he would turn alone to his companions. The second would do the same, then the third, so that the three girls were left by themselves at one end of the room and three young men at the other. And when the third had returned, the first, gambolling and making all

manner of amorous glances, pulling his hose tight and setting his shirt straight, went to claim his damsel, who refused his arm and turned her back on him; then, seeing the young man had returned to his place, she pretended to be in despair. The two others did the same. At last all three went together to claim their respective damsels, and kneeling on the ground, begged this boon with clasped hands, when the damsels fell into their arms and all danced the Courante pell-mell (Kirstein, p. 159).

By the time the coranto reached the English court, the prelude had been dropped. However, this would be fun to stage if the production merited the moment.

2/4 Time	Count	Step to the side diagonally
Measure/bar one	1	L
	&	R
	2	L
Measure/bar two	3	R
	&	L
	4	R
Measure/bar three	5	Run, leap, or glide forward on left foot
	6	Run, leap, or glide forward on the right foot
Measure/bar four	7	L
	&	R
	8	L

Then repeat the whole sequence to the right.

Figure 6.2 Coranto Basic Step

CORANTO

M.M. ♩. = 72

Anon., sixteenth century

Musical Example 6.1   Coranto

Figure 7.1　Galliard

CHAPTER 7
GALLIARD

The Life of King Henry V

Act I, scene ii

AMBASSADOR: Thus, then, in few:
Your Highness, lately sending into France,
Did claim some certain dukedoms in the right
Of your great predecessor, King Edward the Third,
In answer of which claim, the prince our master
Says that you savor too much of your youth,
And bids you be advised: There's naught in France
That can be with a nimble GALLIARD won.

Twelfth Night, or, What You Will

Act I, scene iii

SIR TOBY BELCH: What is thy excellence in a GALLIARD, knight?

SIR ANDREW: Faith, I can cut a caper.[1]

SIR TOBY BELCH: And I can cut the mutton to't.[2]

SIR ANDREW: And I have the back-trick[3] simply as strong as any man in Illyria.

SIR TOBY BELCH: Wherefore are these things hid? Wherefore have these gifts a curtain before 'em? Are they like to take dust, like Mistress Mall's picture? Why dost thou not go to church in a GALLIARD and come home in a coranto? My very walk should be a jig. I would not so much as make water but in a sink-a-pace.[4] What dost thou mean? Is it a world to hide virtues in? I did think, by the excellent constitution of thy leg, it was formed under the star of a GALLIARD.[5]

The galliard is a gay dance with five steps to a phrase, popular in the sixteenth century as a sequel to the stately pavane. It is a dance step achieved by leaping and bringing your calves together in the air, or by clicking your heels together in the air. It may be executed to the front, back, or to either side.

Toby's exit line in Act I, scene iii: "No, sir; it is legs and thighs. Let me see thee caper. Ha, higher; ha, ha, excellent!"

Also in *The Second Part of King Henry the Fourth*, Act i, scene ii, Falstaff states,

My lord, I was born about three of the clock in the afternoon, with a white head and something a round belly. For my voice, I have lost it with hallowing and singing of anthems. To approve my youth further, I

---

[1]Caper: Frolicsome leap. C.T. Prouty, ed. *Twelfth Night, or, What You Will*. In A. Harbage, ed., *The Complete Pelican Shakespeare*. Baltimore: Penguin Books, 1969.

[2]Cut the mutton to't: Toby makes a pun referring to caper sauce. *Shakespeare*, by Hardin Craig.

[3]Back-trick: Some figure in the GALLIARD; apparently, dancing backward. *Shakespeare*, by Hardin Craig.

[4]SINK-A-PACE: The Anglicization of cinque pace, a rapid dance in five steps. It is another name for the galliard.

[5]Under the star of a GALLIARD: A star favorable to dancing. Men's destinies and characters were thought to be controlled by the stars. *Shakespeare*, by Hardin Craig. Galliard: a sixteenth century dance tune in moderately quick triple time with or without an upbeat. *Webster's Third New International Dictionary*.

will not. The truth is, I am only old in judgment and understanding; and that he will CAPER with me for a thousand marks, let him lend me the money, and have at him!

Here Shakespeare means to compete in a dance.

In *Romeo and Juliet*, Mercutio tells Romeo, "You are a lover. Borrow cupid's wings and soar with them above a common bound." By "bound" he means a leap required in some dances, as a caper in a galliard.

Sir Andrew's "back-trick" is probably a back caper: a jump in the air with beating your legs beating together behind you. In ballet terms, this called a capriole. Example: Put your left leg behind you in the air, jump in the air, bring the right leg up to meet the left, and land on the right leg. Keep your legs straight in the jump. Or a back caper could refer to dancing the galliard step while traveling backward.

MUCH ADO ABOUT NOTHING

Act II, scene i

BEATRICE: The fault will be in the music, cousin, if you be not wooed in good time. If the prince be too important, tell him there is measure in everything, and so dance out the answer. For hear me, Hero: wooing, wedding and repenting is a Scotch jig, a measure, and a CINQUE PACE: the first suit is hot and hasty like a Scotch jig (and full as fantastical) ; the wedding, mannerly modest, as a measure, full of state and ancientry; and then comes Repentance and with his bad legs[6] falls into the CINQUE PACE faster and faster, till he sink into his grave.

This was the dance that the Elizabethans made famous. It was sufficiently energetic for Queen Elizabeth I to perform a half a dozen galliards before breakfast as exercise. It was known in France as the gaillarde, and in Italy as the gagliarda, and perhaps derives its name from the Celtic word for strength and prowess. These two qualities were much needed for the dance. Arbeau says that the virtue of the man lies in his agility, precision, rapidity of footwork, and muscular strength. It was the only dance performed bareheaded, hat in hand. The galliard was danced around the hall by couples and groups holding hands. The dancers took turns showing

---

[6]The "bad legs" referred to in Beatrice's speech is an obscure joke, presuming that Shakespeare's audience was familiar with the fashionable dance teaching. It is a reference to Arbeau's description of the cinque pas, a five-step dance that was an antecedent of the galliard, in which the performer is called on to make four "limping hops"—hence the "bad legs." *Let's Dance*, by Peter Buckman.

Figure 7.2   Galliard Basic Step

GALLIARD

Musical Example 7.1   Galliard

off their physical prowess to their partners, other dancers, and the rest of the onlookers. Though known as a couple dance, the galliard came to be virtually a solo for a man, in which he showed off his leaps and jumps, while his partner occasionally performed a step or two while he caught his breath. After a bow and a procession up and down the floor, the couples danced the basic galliard step to each other, around one another, or taking turns. Then the dance got more complicated, with dancers executing steps that included crossing the feet, high and low kicks, forward and backward kicks, and leaps in the air. The dancer might make one or two complete revolutions in the air.

The emphasis was on energy and agility rather than subtlety and restraint. The galliard ceased to be a dance and became an acrobatic feat. It was treated as a sport in England.

It was called the cinq pas (five step) in French and sink-a-pace in English because of its pattern of a syncopated fifth count on the 6th beat.

The tune of "God Save the Queen" (known in the United States as "America, the Beautiful") is a galliard air, as is Verdi's "La donna e mobile."

> The dance is executed in 3/4 time. The last beat is syncopated (hold the 4th beat and syncopate the 5th and 6th). As choreographer Bari Rolfe so simply put it:Hum "My Country 'tis of Thee" (La, La, La, Laaaaa, LaLa).

Sing	My	Coun	try	Tisssss	of		Thee
Or hum	La	La	La	Laaaaa	La		La
Counting beats	1	2	3	4	5	&	6
Step	L	R	L	R Hold		L	R

Footwork
    Count 1—Fall back on the left foot as you kick the right forward
    Count 2—Fall back on the right foot as you kick the left forward
    Count 3—Fall back on the left foot as you kick the right forward
    Count 4—Fall back on the right foot as you kick the left forward
    Count 5—Hold the left foot in the air for the fifth count
    Count 6—Syncopate the count by falling onto the left foot on the
        and count and fall on the right foot on the sixth count.
The step ends with the left foot in the air.

To do the backward galliard, dancers fall forward on the left foot and do the sequence falling forward.

There was a milder version of the galliard called the tordion (stepping back on the left foot and pointing the right toe without falling or kicking). It had the same timing as the galliard and was danced by the elderly. It eliminated the jumps, and the tempos were more moderate. And then, of course, there was an even more rambunctious galliard called la volta.

These dances required the qualities of exhibitionism and skill that Good Queen Bess encouraged. It did not long survive her.

Peter Warlock has orchestrated six of the more danceable tunes in his *Capriol Suite*, which gives a good idea of the atmosphere of sixteenth-century dancing. There is also a recording by Archiv Produktion called *Golden Dance Hits of 1600* that captures the spirit of the galliard.

Figure 8.1   Jig

CHAPTER 8
JIG (GIGUE)

Act II, scene ii

HAMLET: It shall to the barber's, with your beard. Prithee, say on: he's for a JIG[1] or a tale of bawdry, or he sleeps: say on: come to Hecuba.

Act III, scene i

HAMLET: I have heard of your paintings too, well enough; God has given you one face, and you make yourselves another: you JIG, you amble and you lisp, and nick-name God's creatures, and you make wantonness your ignorance. Go to, I'll no more on't; it hath made me mad. I say, we will have no more marriages: those that are married already—all but one —shall live. The rest shall keep as they are. To a nunnery, go.

HAMLET: O God, your only JIG-Maker! What should a man do but be merry? For look you how cheerfully my mother looks, and my father died within's two hours.

---

[1]JIG('jig) *n* -s [prob. Fr. MF giguer to dance, jig, gambol about, frolic, gigue fiddle, of Gmc origin; akin to OHG giga fiddle; akin to ON geiga to turn aside—more at GIG] 1a: any of several lively springy dances in triple rhythm, popular in 16th and 17th century England and Scotland and still commonly danced in Ireland in a way characterized by intricate and dexterous motions of the feet; b: music by which a jig may be danced; c: GIGUE; d: a rapid usu. jerky up and down or to and fro motion. *Webster's Third New International Dictionary.*

LOVE'S LABOUR'S LOST

Act III, scene i

   MOTH: No, my complete master; but to JIG off a tune at the tongue's
   end, canary to it with your feet, humor it with turning up your eyelids,
   sigh a note and sing a note, sometime through the throat as if you swal-
   lowed love with singing love, sometime through the nose as if you
   snuffed up love by smelling love; with your hat penthouse-like o'er the
   shop of your eyes; with your arms crossed on your thin-belly doublet
   like a rabbit on a spit; or your hands in your pocket like a man after the
   old painting; and keep not too long in one tune, but snip and away.
   These are complements, these are humours, these betray nice wenches
   (that would be betrayed without these), and make them men of
   note—do you note me?—that are most affected to these.

Act IV, scene iii

   BEROWNE: O what a scene of fool'ry I have seen,
   Of sighs, of groans, of sorrow, and of teen!
   O me, with what strict patience have I sat,
   To see a king transformed to a gnat;
   To see great Hercules whipping a gig,
   And profound Solomon to tune a JIG[2]
   And Nestor play a push-pin with the boys,
   And critic Timon laugh at idle toys!

---

[2]Tune a jig: To sing a rhyme. A. Harbage, ed. *Love's Labour's Lost.* In A. Harbage, ed., *The Complete Pelican Shakespeare,* Baltimore: Penguin Books, 1969.

MUCH ADO ABOUT NOTHING

Act II, scene i

BEATRICE: The fault will be in the music, cousin, if you be not wooed in good time. If the prince be too important, tell him there is measure in everything, and so dance out the answer. For, hear me, Hero: wooing, wedding, and repenting is a Scotch JIG, a measure, and a cinque pace: the first suit is hot and hasty like a Scotch JIG (and full as fantastical); the wedding, mannerly modest, as a measure, full of state and ancientry; and then comes Repentance and with his bad legs falls into the cinque pace faster and faster, till he sink into his grave.

TWELFTH NIGHT, OR, WHAT YOU WILL

Act I, scene iii

SIR TOBY BELCH: Wherefore are these things hid? Wherefore have these gifts a curtain before 'em? Are they like to take dust, like Mistress Mall's picture? Why dost thou not go to church in a galliard and come home in a coranto? My very walk should be a JIG. I would not so much as make water but in a sink-a-pace. What dost thou mean? Is it a world to hide virtues in? I did think, by the excellent constitution of thy leg, it was formed under the star of a galliard.

The jig is a country dance, mainly associated with Ireland but known throughout Europe. The jig was the exception to the rule that country dances were always danced in groups. It was an opportunity for a couple to dance one on one. In the sixteenth century it was a solo dance, a forerunner of the galliard. The French called it a gigue and toned it down to become part of a courtly suite. It also became a stage dance used to conclude a play. One example was Kemp's Jigge, named after William Kemp, a comic actor who appeared with Shakespeare in many of his plays and who was also known for the jigs with which he concluded his performances. His jig is referred to as a theatrical dance. John Playford, in his *The English Dancing Master*, describe Kemp's jig as follows (it's a round for six [three men and three women]):

PART I

One man lead in two women forward and back:

Honour to one, honour to the other, then turn the third:

Lead your own with the left hand, and the woman you turned, and as much:

Then as much with the other second woman, turning your own:

The next man as much: Then the third as much:

PART II

First man lead the woman as before: turn half round holding both hands, and his own as much to the other, turn the third woman. Do thus to all, the rest following and doing the like.

PART III

First man take the woman as before by the contrary hands behind, then lead them forwards and back, pull one half about and kiss her, as much with the other, then the third. Do thus to all, the rest following and doing the like (Playford, p. 25).

Translation (methinks):

PART I

Man #1 leads woman #1 and woman #2 downstage and back upstage and bows to one then to the other. Then man #1 gives woman #3 his left hand and gives her an underarm turn (she turns to her left), and then he turns on his own (to his right). He then turns woman #2. Then turns woman #1. Man #2 repeats the same pattern with woman #2, woman #3, and woman #1. Man #3 repeats the same pattern with woman #3, woman #1, and woman #2.

PART II

Man #1 leads woman #1 downstage and back. Taking both hands, they turn half a circle to the left, exchanging places. He repeats this with woman #2 and again with woman #3. Man #2 does the same with woman #2 and repeats pattern with woman #3 and woman #1. Man #3 repeats the pattern with woman #3, woman #1, and woman #2.

Figure 8.2 Kemp's Jigge

PART III

Man #1 brings woman #1 forward and back, holding hands behind. Her right hand is in his right hand, and her left hand in his left hand. He then lets go of her and pulls her to him for a kiss. He repeats this with woman #2 and again with woman #3. All the men repeat the pattern with their partners and the other women. They are jigging (stepping or hopping) on every beat of the music.

The basic jig I learned as a boy started in fifth position (feet turned out with right foot in front of the left). Count 1—hop on the left foot, bringing the right foot (pointed) in front, shin height. Count 2—hop again on the left foot, bringing the right foot behind at the calf. Count 3—hop and land on both feet with left foot in front. On counts 4, 5, 6, repeat to the other side by starting the hop on the right foot.

The arms: Raise the arm with the alternate leg. Example: Left arm held over the head while the right foot is doing the beats on the shin, then the calf. Change arms when you change to the other side.

This step can be done traveling front, back, leaping to the side, and turning. It is an up-and-down movement done in all directions. Couples start facing each other, moving from and toward their partner. They may dance around each other or back to back, moving in opposite directions. The patterns are up to the choreographer or the design of a known jig.

The jig is danced in 3/4, 6/8, 9/9, and 12/8 time. Don't count, just jig! But count if you are designing a dance, of course.

Beat
1
2
3
Prepare
Repeat
Other Side

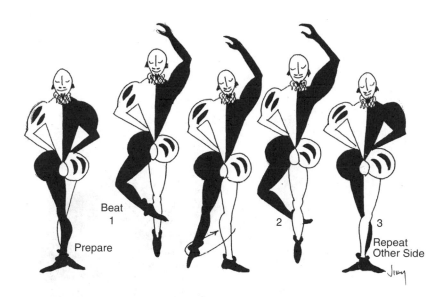

Figure 8.3 Jig Basic Step

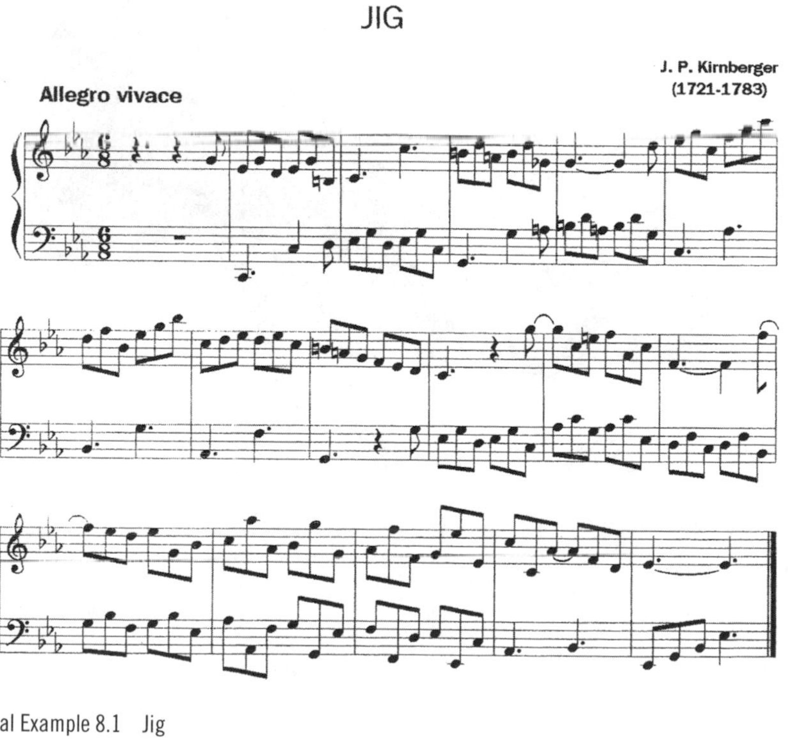

JIG
J. P. Kirnberger
(1721-1783)
Allegro vivace

Musical Example 8.1 Jig

Figure 9.1   La Volta

Chapter 9
La Volta

The Life of King Henry V

Act III, scene v

DUKE OF BOURBON: They bid us to the English dancing schools
And teach LAVOLTAS[1] high, and swift corantos,
Saying our grace is only in our heels
And that we are most lofty runaways.

---

[1]La volta (here, lavolta) Dance characterized by leaps; la volta meaning to turn. *The Complete Pelican Shakespeare*, edited by Alfred Harbage.

THE HISTORY OF TROILUS AND CRESSIDA

Act IV, scene iii

> TROILUS: Die I a villain, then!
> In this I do not call your faith in question
> So mainly as my merit. I cannot sing,
> Nor heel the high LAVOLT[2], nor sweeten talk,
> Nor play at subtle games—fair virtues all,
> To which the Grecians are most prompt and pregnant;
> But I can tell that in each grace of these
> There lurks a still and dumb—discoursive devil
> That tempts most cunningly. But be not tempted.

The orchestra strikes up the music in a 3/4 cadence. The dancers hop, turn, step; then the man lifts his lady high in the air, boosting her with his thigh while holding onto her waist and corset. He turns her in the air. The lady squeals and tries desperately to hold her gown down so that the court does not get a glimpse of her undergarments or a flash of her bare leg.

That is La Volta—a sixteenth-century dance probably born in northern Italy. The word "volta" means "turning dance." Because of the closeness of the partners and the fact that men lifted the ladies high in the air, the dance was considered by the moralists of the day to be immoral and highly indecent. It was a great favorite of Queen Elizabeth I.

La Volta is a form of the galliard. The couple face each other, holding each other closely. On count 1, the man hops back on his left foot, turning back to his left. On count 2, he continues turning back with a bigger step pivoting on his right. On count 3, he bends his knees and sweeps the lady into the air. He places his right arm around her waist and his left hand on the front of her busk (corset). He turns her in the air for the next two measures and gently places her down on the fourth measure. To keep from getting too dizzy, he may turn her to the other side by reversing the steps.

The lady places her left arm around the man's shoulder or neck as she hops forward on her right foot on count 1. She continues forward on her left foot (count 2) as she bends her knees and prepares to lift (count 3). Her right arm is thrust into the air, or holds her skirts down if she is the modest

---

[2]Lavolt: A lively dance. V.K. Whitaker, ed. *The History of Troilus and Cressida*. In A. Harbage, ed., *The Complete Pelican Shakespeare*. Baltimore: Penguin Books, 1969.

sort. The movement is very much like a groom sweeping up his bride to carry her across the threshold. The difference is that the dancer has to step in time to the music and keep turning once he gets her up there, his arms

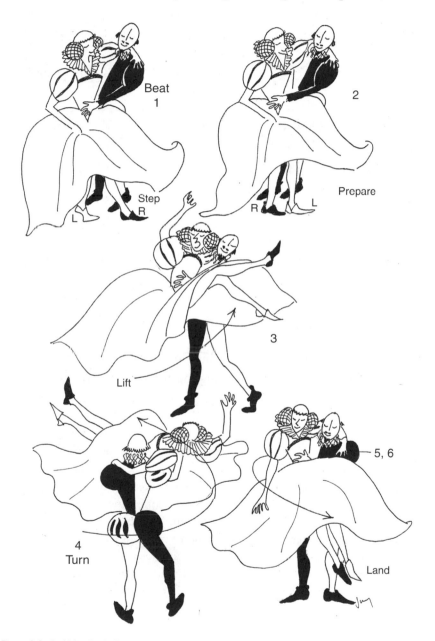

Figure 9.2 La Volta Basic Step with Lift

LA VOLTA

William Byrd

Musical Example 9.1   La Volta

around her waist and on her stomach. For all this, the gallant is rewarded a kiss. I trust the groom is rewarded a bit more.

In the sixteenth century, the dancing master Thoinot Arbeau issued a warning to the men:

> After having turned by as many cadences as you please, restore the damsel to her place where she will feel, no matter what good countenance she makes, her head whirling, full of vertigo and giddiness, and perhaps you will feel the same. I leave you to judge whether it be a proper thing for a young girl to make large steps and wide movements of the legs. And whether in this VOLTA her honor and well-being are not risked and involved. Nowadays dancers lack these courteous considerations in their VOLTAS and other similarly wanton and wayward dances that have been brought into usage. In dancing them the damsels are made to bounce about in such a fashion that more often than not they show their bare knees unless they keep one hand on their skirt to prevent it (Buckman, p. 91).

His student Capriol comments, "This manner of dancing seems neither beautiful nor honorable to me unless one is dancing with some strapping hussy from the servant's hall" (Arbeau, M.S. Evans, trans., p. 87).

If I were a strapping hussy from the servant's hall, I'd resent that.

A version of La Volta can be seen in the film *The Sword and the Rose.* The film was made in 1953 with Richard Todd and Glynis Johns. It is available on video.

Figure 10.1   Measure/Pavan

CHAPTER 10
MEASURE/PAVAN

ALL'S WELL THAT ENDS WELL

Act II, scene ii

PAROLLES: Use a more spacious ceremony to the noble lords, you have restrained yourself within the list of too cold an adieu. Be more expressive to them; for they wear themselves in the cap of the time; there do muster true gait, eat, speak, and move under the influence of the most received star; and though the devil lead the MEASURE[1], such are to be followed. After them, and take a more dilated farewell.

AS YOU LIKE IT

Act V, scene iv

TOUCHSTONE: If any man doubt that, let him put me to my purgation. I have trod a MEASURE; I have flattered a lady; I have been politic with my friend, smooth with mine enemy; I have undone three tailors; I have had four quarrels, And like to have fought one.

---

[1]Measure: 4a: something having rhythmic sound or movement. (1): melody, tune. (2): a round or turn of dancing: dance. (3): a slow and stately dance. (4): rhythmic structure: measured pattern of movement. (5): beat, cadence, musical time. (6): a division or unit (as of time or stress) in a rhythmic sequence. *Webster's Third New Internatiomal Dictionary.*

Act V, scene iv

  DUKE SENIOR: Welcome, young man.
  Thou offer'st fairly to thy brothers' wedding:
  To one, his lands withheld; and to the other,
  A land itself at large, a potent dukedom.
  First, in this forest let us do those ends
  That here we well begun and well begot;
  And after, every of this happy number
  That have endured shrewd days and nights with us
  Shall share the good of our returned fortune,
  According to the measure of their states.
  Meantime forget this new-fall'n dignity
  And fall into our rustic revelry.
  Play, music, and you brides and bridegrooms all,
  With MEASURE heaped in joy, to th' MEASURES fall.

Act V, scene iv

  JAQUES (To Touchstone):
  And you to wrangling, for thy loving voyage
  Is but for two months victualled. So, to your pleasures:
  I am for other than for dancing MEASURES.

THE LIFE OF KING HENRY VIII

Act I, scene iv

  KING: Lead in your ladies ev'ry one. Sweet partner,
  I must not foresake you. Let's be merry,
  Good my lord cardinal; I have a dozen healths
  To drink to these fair ladies, and a MEASURE
  To lead 'em once again; and then let's dream
  Who's best in favor. Let the music knock it.
  [Exit with trumpets]

LOVE'S LABOUR'S LOST

Act V, scene ii

  KING: Say to her, we have measured many miles,
  To tread a MEASURE with her on the grass.

BOYET: They say that they have measured many a mile
To tread a MEASURE with you on the grass.

ROSALINE: It is not so. Ask them how many inches
Is in one mile. If they have measured many,
The measure then of one is easily told.

BOYET: If to come hither you have measured miles,
And many miles, the princess bids you tell
How many inches doth fill up one mile.

BEROWNE: Tell her we measure them by weary steps.

BOYET: She hears herself.

ROSALINE: How many weary steps,
Of many weary miles you have o'ergone
Are numb'red in the travel of one mile?

BEROWNE: We number nothing that we spend for you.
Our duty is so rich, so infinite,
That we may do it still without accompt.
Vouchsafe to show the sunshine of your face,
That we, like savages, may worship it.

ROSALINE: My face is but a moon, and clouded too.

KING: Blessed are clouds, to as such clouds do.
Vouchsafe, bright moon, and these thy stars, to shine
Those clouds removed, upon our watery eyne.

ROSALINE: O vain petitioner, beg a greater matter!
Thou now requests but moonshine in the water.

KING: Then in our MEASURE do but vouchsafe one change.
Thou bid'st me beg; this begging is not strange.

ROSALINE: Play, music, then. Nay, you must do it soon.
[Music plays]
Not yet—no dance! Thus chance I like the moon.
KING: Will you not dance? How come you thus enstranged?

ROSALINE: You took the moon at full, but now she's changed.

KING: Yet still she is the moon, and I the man.
The music plays; vouchsafe some motion to it.

ROSALINE: Our ears vouchsafe it.

KING: But your legs should do it.

ROSALINE: Since you are strangers and come here by chance,
We'll not be nice: take hands—we will not dance.

KING: Why take we hands then?

ROSALINE: Only to part friends.
Curtsy, sweet hearts; and so the MEASURE ends.

KING: More measure of this MEASURE! Be not nice.

ROSALINE: We can afford no more at such a price.

KING: Price you yourselves. What buys your company?

ROSALINE: Your absence only.

KING: That can never be.

ROSALINE: Then cannot we be bought; and so adieu—
Twice to your visor, and half once to you.

KING: If you deny to dance, let's hold more chat.

ROSALINE: In private then.

KING: I am best pleased with that.

MUCH ADO ABOUT NOTHING

Act II, scene i

BEATRICE: The fault will be in the music, cousin, if you be not wooed in good time. If the prince be too important, tell him there is measure in everything, and so dance out the answer. For hear me, Hero: wooing, wedding and repenting is a Scotch jig, a MEASURE, and a cinque pace: the first suit is hot and hasty like a Scotch jig (and full as fantastical); the wedding, mannerly modest, as a MEASURE, full of state and ancientry; and then comes Repentance and with his bad legs falls into the cinque pace faster and faster, till he sink into his grave.

PERICLES, PRINCE OF TYRE

Act II, scene iii

KING: Now, by the gods, I pity his misfortune
And will awake him from his melancholy.
Come, gentleman, we sit too long on trifles
And waste the time that looks for other revels.
Even in your armors, as you are addressed,
Will you well become a soldier's.
I will not have an excuse with saying this:
Loud music is too loud for ladies' heads,
Since they love men in arms as well as beds.
[They dance]
So, this was well asked, 'twas so well performed.
Come, sir.
Here is a lady that wants breathing too;
And I have heard, you knights of Tyre
Are excellent in making ladies trip,
And that their MEASURES are as excellent.

PERICLES: In those that practice they are, my lord.

KING: O, that's as much as you would be denied
Of your fair courtesy,
[They dance] Unclasp, unclasp!
Thanks, gentlemen, to all; all have done well,
[To Pericles]
But you the best. Pages and lights to conduct
These Knights unto their several lodgings!
Yours, sir, We have given order to be next our own.

PERICLES: I am at your grace's pleasure.

KING: Princes, it is too late to talk of love;
And that's the mark I know you level at.
Therefore each one betake him to his rest;
To-morrow all for speedng do their best.
[Exeunt]

THE TRAGEDY OF KING RICHARD II

Act I, scene iii

GAUNT: All places that the eye of heaven visits
Are to a wise man ports and happy havens.
Teach thy necessity to reason thus:
There is no virtue like necessity.
Think not the king did banish thee,
But thou the king. Woe doth the heavier sit
Where it perceives it is but faintly borne.
Go, say I sent thee forth to purchase honor,
And not the king exiled thee; or suppose
Devouring pestilence hangs in our air
And thou art flying to a fresher clime.
Look what thy soul holds dear, imagine it
To lie that way thou goest, not whence thou com'st.
Suppose the singing birds musicians,
The grass whereon thy tread'st the presence strewed,
The flowers fair ladies, and thy steps no more
Than a delightful MEASURE or a dance;
For gnarling sorrow hath less power to bite
The man that mocks at it and sets it light.

Act III, scene iv

[Enter the Queen and two ladies, her attendants]
QUEEN: What sport shall we devise here in this garden
To drive away the heavy thought of care?

LADY: Madam, we'll play at bowls.

QUEEN: 'Twill make me think the world is full of rubs
And that my fortune runs against the bias.

LADY: Madam, we'll dance.

QUEEN: My legs can keep no MEASURE in delight
When my poor heart no MEASURE keeps in grief.
Therefore no dancing, girl; some other sport.

The Tragedy of King Richard III

Act I, scene i

   [Enter Richard, Duke of Gloucester, solus]
   RICHARD: Now is the winter of our discontent
   Made glorious summer by this son of York;
   And all the clouds that lowered upon our house
   In the deep bosom of the ocean buried.
   Now are our brows bound with victorious wreaths,
   Our bruised arms hung up for monuments,
   Our stern alarums changed to merry meetings,
   Our dreadful marches to delightful MEASURES.
   Grim-visaged war hath smoothed his wrinkled front,
   And now, instead of mounting barbed steeds
   To fright the souls of fearful adversaries,
   He capers nimbly in a lady's chamber
   To the lascivious pleasing of a lute.
   But I, that am not shaped for sportive tricks
   Nor made to court an amorous looking-glass;
   I, that am curtailed of this fair proportion,
   Cheated of feature by dissembling Nature,
   Deformed, unfinished, sent before my time
   Into this breathing world, scarce half made up,
   And that so lamely and unfashionable
   That dogs bark at me as I halt by them—
   Why I, in this weak piping time of peace,
   Have no delight to pass away the time,
   Unless to see my shadow in the sun
   And descant on mine own deformity.
   And therefore, since I cannot prove a lover
   To entertain these fair well-spoken days,
   I am determined to prove a villain
   And hate the idle pleasures of these days.
   Plots have I laid, inductions dangerous,
   By drunken prophecies, libels, and dreams,
   To set my brother Clarence and the king

In deadly hate the one against the other;
And if King Edward be as true and just
As I am subtle, false, and treacherous,
This day should Clarence closely be mewed up
About a prophecy which says that "G"
Of Edward's heirs the murderer shall be.
Dive, thoughts, down to my soul—here Clarence comes!

ROMEO AND JULIET

Act I, scene iv

BENVOLIO: The date is out of such prolixity.
We'll have no Cupid hoodwinked with a scarf,
Bearing a Tartar's painted bow of lath,
Scaring the ladies like a crowkeeper;
Nor no without-book prologue, faintly spoke
After the prompter, for our entrance;
But, let them measure us by what they will,
We'll MEASURE them a MEASURE and be gone.

Act I, scene iv

ROMEO: O, she doth teach the torches to burn bright!
It seems she hangs upon the cheek of night
As a rich jewel in an Ethiop's ear—
Beauty too rich for use, for earth too dear!
So shows a snowy dove trooping with crows
As yonder lady o'er her fellows shows.
The MEASURE done, I'll watch her place of stand
And, touching hers, make blessed my rude hand.
Did my heart love till now? Foreswear it, sight!
For I ne'er saw true beauty till this night.

TWELFTH NIGHT, OR, WHAT YOU WILL

Act V, scene i

CLOWN: Primo, secundo, tertio is a good play; and the old saying is
"The third pays for all." The triplex, sir, is a good tripping MEASURE; or
the bells of Saint Bennet, sir, may put you in mind—one, two, three.

Act V, scene i

CLOWN: O, he's drunk, Sir Toby, an hour agone. His eyes were set at eight i' th' morning.

SIR TOBY: Then he's a rogue and a passy measure PAVIN.[2] I hate a drunken rogue.

What the Elizabethans called the measure was known elsewhere as the basse dance. It dates from the fourteenth century. When Thoinot Arbeau wrote *Orchesography* in 1589, he stated the basse dance had been out of date for forty or fifty years. But he also said, "I foresee that wise and dignified matrons will restore it to fashion as being a type of dance full of virtue and decorum (Arbeau, M. S. Evans, trans., p. 51)." The name basse meant that the feet were kept close to the ground as opposed to haute, which meant to jump and hop.

The measure (basse danse) music is written in 3/4 time and in even four-bar phrases. The dance itself is made up of (1) the reverence (bow or curtsey), (2) the branle (sway), (3) the simples (single step), (4) the double (two steps), (5) the reprise (bending the knees to one side or the other), and (6) the conge (returning your partner from whence you found her). It is a very smooth, grand, and stately dance. Every movement takes a full measure of music. Capriol, Arbeau's student, asked the master, "How shall I execute these movements when I wish to dance a basse dance?" Arbeau answers,

> In the first you will choose some comely damsel who takes your fancy, and, removing your hat or bonnet with your left hand, proffer her your right to lead her out to dance. She, being sensible and well brought up, will offer you her left hand. Then you will conduct her to the end of the room and give notice to the musicians to play a basse dance. And when they begin to play you will begin to dance (Arbeau, M. S. Evans, trans., p. 51).

(1) The reverence: Men bow and women curtsey. Step backward and bend your knees as if you were going to kneel. The man doffs his hat as he bows and replaces it as he stands. Each move takes three beats: stepping

---

[2]Pavanne (pa van, -van, also pavan or pavin, 'pavan) *n.* -s [MF pavane, fr. Osp pavana, fr oit, prob, alter. Of padovana, fem of padovano of Padua, city in NE Italy, fr Padova Padua + ano -an [fr. L-anus]: 1. A stately court dance by couples in ceremonial costume introduced from Southern Europe into England in the 16th century; 2a: Music for the pavane; b: Music having the duple and slow stately rhythm of the pavane. *Webster's Third New International Dictionary.*

A MESURE

Set for Keyboard by Arnold Dolmetsch
M.M. o = 48

Giles Lodge Lute Book, 1570

Musical Example 10.1   A Measure

back (1, 2, 3), bending knees (1, 2, 3), straightening the knees (1, 2, 3), and closing the feet to first position (heels together, toes turned out comfortably) (1, 2, 3). So the entire bow takes four measures, or bars, of music. After the bow, the dancers face the same direction. The lady is on the man's right side. He holds up his right hand, and the lady places her hand on his.

(2) The branle: Like the reverence, it needs four bars of music.

Measure one: On the 1st and 2nd beat do nothing. On the 3rd beat of the measure, raise up on your toes.

Measure two: On the 1st beat, put your weight on the outside foot (man's left, woman's right), slightly bend your knees, and turn away from your partner. Stay put on the 2nd beat. On the 3rd beat, up on your toes and face front again.

Measure three: Beat 1, same as 1st beat, measure two, only, this time, instead of looking away from your partner, look over your shoulder at each other. Stay put on the 2nd beat. On the 3rd beat, rise up on your toes and face forward.

Measure four: 1st beat, lower both heels together. 2nd and 3rd beats, do nothing (smile or chitchat maybe).

(3) The simples: Two simples are needed to fill out a two-measure phrase.

Measure one: 1st beat, step forward on the left foot, a bit on the diagonal, bowing slightly to the left. Hold 2nd and 3rd beats.

Measure two: Bring the right foot to the left and rise up on your toes. Hold 2nd and 3rd beats. That is one simple (single). To fill out the phrase (four measures), repeat the first two measures, stepping out on the right foot.

(4) The double: The double needs four measures of music.

Measure one: 1st beat, step forward on the ball of the left foot, weight always forward. Hold 2nd and 3rd beats.

Measure two: 1st beat, step forward with the right foot passing the left foot. Hold 2nd and 3rd beats.

Measure three: Step forward with the left foot passing the right foot.

Measure four: Bring the right foot to the left and lower the heels. Hold 2nd and 3rd beats.

(5) The reprise: Each movement takes four bars or measures.

Measure one: On the 1st beat, take a small step back with the right foot. Hold 2nd and 3rd beats.

Measure two: On the 1st beat, make a small bow to the left side. Hold 2nd and 3rd beats.

Measure three: On the 1st beat, raise the body while again facing front. Hold 2nd and 3rd beats.

Measure four: On the 1st beat, bring the left foot back to meet the right in first position, and hold 2nd and 3rd beats.

If you repeated the reprise you would start on the left foot. It is like bowing from side to side.

6) The conge: When the dance has ended the man bows to his lady, takes her by the hand, and returns her to the place from which they started the dance.

These steps can be done in various order depending on the specific dance. Each basse dance was named and was danced in a specific manner. La Basse Danse de Bourgogne and La Dame are two examples explained in detail in Melusine Wood's book, *Historical Dances 12th to 19th Century*.

Figure 10.2   Reverence/Branle

Being such a slow dance, the measure left a lot of time for flirting and chatting as dancers grandly moved from one end of the hall to the other.

In *The Book of the Dance*, Lincoln Kirstein states, "The PAVANNE, PAVIN, PANICIN or by what other variants one recognizes it, derives its name from either the town of Padua or Pavo (French paon) a peacock, from the manner in which ladies swept their long trains or from one of its figures, where the dancers are arranged in a circle in the manner of a peacock

Simple (Single)

Beat
1

2

Settle on
3
Repeat on
Other Side

Double

Beat
1

2

3

Settle
1, 2, 3
Repeat on
Other Side

Figure 10.3 Simple (Single)/Double

spreading its tail. . . . The PAVANNE was popular all over Europe. Italy, France and Spain claim it as a national dance. There was a French term 'en se pavenant' which means 'strutting like a peacock,' or more technically, 'to step as in PAVANNES'" (Kirstein, p. 158). The English composer Peter Warlock has orchestrated six of the more danceable tunes in his *Capriol Suite*.

At court, the pavan was the first dance of the evening and was very processional. After the pavan there usually came a galliard. With the pavan and galliard played and danced back to back, the music would go from a slow

Reprise

Beat 1

2, 3

1

2, 3

Reverence

Figure 10.4   Reprise/Reverence

4/4 or 2/2 to a quick 3/4. Thus came the birth of what was to become known as the Suite.

In *Twelfth Night,* Shakespeare refers to the "passy measure pavin." According to Louis Horst in *Pre-Classic Dance Forms,* passy measures is a corruption of passamezzo, an Italian variant of the pavane. *Grove's Dictionary* states that the passamezzo was, "an old Italian dance which was probably a variety of the PAVANE" (Horst, p. 13). In England, where it

BASSE DANSE

Recoup
M.M.♩ = 64

Musical Example 10.2   Basse Danse

was popular during Queen Elizabeth I's time, it was known as "passing measures pavan." Arbeau says that the musicians played the pavan less gravely, and "in this manner it partakes of the moderate tempo of a Basse-dance, when it is called passemezzo" (Horst, p. 111). Mabel Dolmetsch (Horst, p. 111) is probably more correct when she says the pavan differs from the passamezzo in the proportion of steps taken to the music. A step that would take one bar of music in the pavan would take two steps in the passamezzo, and the music would be played faster. So when Shakespeare's clown in *Twelfth Night* refers to a passy measure pavin, he means a pavan with a faster tempo.

The pavan is very easy to execute. It is very similar to the wedding march a bride takes down the aisle or the walk a stripper takes down the runway . . . with a variation or two.

Couples are side by side, the lady on the right of the man. A reverence (bow) is made. He extends his hand, and she places her hand, palm up, upon his. His thumb is holding her hand in place. Her other hand is to her side or touching her farthingale. He rests his hand on his hip. They step left, touch right (simple), step right to touch left (simple), and a

THE EARL OF SALISBURY'S PAVAN

I.M. ♩ = 56

William Byrd

Musical Example 10.3   The Earl of Salisbury's Pavan

double: walk left, right, left, and they touch. On the touch, they rise up on their toes and repeat on the other side. Those eight bars are then repeated going backward. The steps are taken to the diagonal, with the rise to the toes coming on the second beat when doing a single and on the 4th beat when doing a double.

This is a very basic step. Many variations can be choreographed into the dance. Sometimes the pavan is done with the couples following a head couple down the center of the hall, or with two or three couples going down the floor abreast of each other. It was grand, stately, and strutted, as we say, like a peacock.

Figure 11.1   Morris Dance

CHAPTER 11
MORRIS DANCE

ALL'S WELL THAT ENDS WELL

Act II, scene ii

LAVATCH: As fit as ten goats is for the hand of an attorney, as your French crown for your taffeta punk, as Tib's rush for Tom's forefinger, as a pancake for Shrove Tuesday, A MORRIS[1] for May day, as the nail to his hole, the cuckold to his horn, as a scolding queen to a wrangling knave, as the nun's lip to the friar's mouth, nay, as the pudding to his skin.

---

[1]Morris dance: *n.* pl morrises or morrices; [ME moreys daunce, Fr. Moreys, morys Moorish + daunce dance] 1: a vigorous dance done by men wearing costumes and bells and carrying sticks or handkerchiefs and performed as a traditional part of English pageants, processions, and May Day games, often by a group of six men plus solo dancers who represent traditional characters. 2: a lively and rhythmic movement suggestive to a morris. *Webster's Third New International Dictionary.*

The Life of King Henry V

Act II, scene iv

    DAUPHIN: My most redoubted father,
It is most meet we arm us 'gainst the foe:
For peace itself should not so dull a kingdom
Though war nor no known quarrel were in question
But that defenses, musters, preparations
Should be maintained, assembled, and collected,
As were a war in expectation.
Therefore, I say 'tis meet we all go forth
To view the sick and feeble parts of France:
and let us do it with no show of fear;
No, with no more than if we heard that England
Were busied with a Whitsun[2] MORRIS DANCE:
For, my good liege, she is so idly king'd,
Her sceptre so fantastically borne
By a vain, giddy, shallow, humorous youth,
That fear attends her not.

A Midsummer Night's Dream

Act II, scene i

    TITANIA: The ox hath therefore stretched its yoke in vain,
The ploughman lost his sweat, and the green corn
Hath rotted ere his youth attained a beard;
The fold stands empty in the drowned field,
And crows are fatted with the murrion flock;
The nine men's MORRIS is filled up with mud;
And the quaint mazes in the wanton green
For lack of tread are undistinguishable.

---

[2]Whitsun festival week beginning the seventh Sunday after Easter (or Whitsunday, which is celebrated in the Christian calendar as Pentecost). A. Harbage, ed. *The Life of King Henry the Fifth*. In A. Harbage, ed., *The Complete Pelican Shakespeare*. Baltimore: Penguin Books, 1969.

The Second Part of King Henry VI

Act III, scene i

YORK: In Ireland have I seen this stubborn Cade
Oppose himself against a troop of kerns,
And fought so long till that his thighs with darts
Were almost like a sharp-quilled porpentine;
And in the end being rescued, I have seen
Him caper upright like a wild MORISCO[3],
Shaking the bloody darts as he his bells.

[3]Morisco: Morris dancer. R.K. Turner, Jr. and G.W. Williams, eds. *The Second and Third Parts of King Henry the Sixth*. In A. Harbage, ed., *The Complete Pelican Shakespeare*. Baltimore: Penguin Books, 1969.

THE FIRST PART OF KING HENRY IV

Act III, scene iii

> FALSTAFF: There's no more faith in thee than in a stewed prune, nor
> no more truth in thee than in a drawn fox; and for womenhood, Maid
> Marian[4] may be the deputy's wife of the ward to thee. Go, you thing, go!

In *Much Ado About Nothing*, Benedick says to Leonato, "Yet is this no
charm for the toothache. Old signior, walk aside with me. I have studied
eight or nine wise words to speak to you, which these hobby-horses must
not hear." By hobbyhorses, Shakespeare meant buffoons. Orginally they
were antic, grotesque figures in a morris dance.

In Peter Buckman's book *Let's Dance* (p. 271), the glossary of dance
defines morris dance as "an English folk dance dating back to pre-Chris-
tian times, primarily a dance of regeneration, and performed by two files of
dancers, usually six in each number, equipped with bells and ribbons."

The origins of morris dancing are not really known. By Shakespeare's
time the dances were already considered an old English custom, dating
back as early as fourteenth century. Some say the dance got its name from
the Moorish captives brought to England by the Crusaders. Others state
that John of Gaunt, Duke of Lancaster, returned to England with Spanish
Moors as captives. There is a slight connection with the Italian moresque.
If you recall Franco Zefferelli's 1968 film *Romeo and Juliet*, he had the
dancers in the Capulet party scene call for and dance the moresque. They
began to ring small bells attached to their costumes and danced a slow
cadence in a circle as Romeo stalked Juliet as she danced. In his *Sports and
Pastimes of the People of England*, Joseph Strutt doubts that the moresque
was the origin: "The Morisco or Moor dance is exceedingly different from
the morris-dance, being performed with castanets, or rattles at the end of
the fingers, and not with bells being attached to various parts of the dress"
(*Go Britannia! Travel Guide*). Strutt goes on to suggest that the morris
dance originated from the "fool's dance" (fourteenth century), in which
the dancers dressed in the manner of the court fool, and from which can
be traced the bells used by morris dancers. Then again it might be derived
from the game "merelles," forms of which were called ninepenny morris or

---

[4]Maid Marian: Disreputable woman in morris dances. M.A. Shaaber, ed. *The First Part of King Henry
the Fourth*. In A. Harbage, ed., *The Complete Pelican Shakespeare*. Baltimore: Penguin Books, 1969.

nine men's morris, referred to in *A Midsummer Night's Dream* by Titania, Act II, scene i. On the Continent, the name was applied to the stepping, dance-like game of hopscotch. In some English morrises, the dancers disguise their faces with soot, which caused them to have a Moorish appearance. This strengthens the argument for a Spanish Moor origin.

In the very beginning it is said that the morris dance was a pantomime of war, representing the Moors' struggle with Christianity. It was a dance of celebration, a reenactment of the battles and performed on May Day by hundreds of people. Eventually the pantomime settled down and became a very popular group dance around 1500. *StreetSwing.com Dance History Archives* says in the early history of the dance there seemed to be three types of morris: (1) a solo dance performed at Moorish courts with stamping feet along with heel stamps; (2) a couple or group dance, which usually portrayed (sword) combat; and (3) a large-scale dance that utilized one to two hundred people in two groups, dancing and acting out a battle pantomime.

The English introduced other costumed characters in Morris dances to celebrate May Day: the foreman of the Morris, the bavian (a fool), a boy dressed as Maid Marian, and the musician. They were followed by Robin Hood, Friar Tuck, Little John, and the Merry Men of Sherwood. They all danced while clashing their staves and jiggling the bells attached to their garters.

The English also made it more of a dance than a celebration by adding the bells, handkerchiefs, hobbyhorses, sticks, and sooted faces to make the dance more distinctive.

The steps and patterns were very complex, and a constant jog-trot movement was maintained throughout the dance. Six to nine dancers go through an orderly maze of intricate steps accompanied by a one-man band who played a flute, bagpipe, violin, accordion, and tabor. The music was beat out on the little drum in 2/4 time.

Thoinot Arbeau describes the basic step:

> The dancer keeps the tips of his toes rigid and close together *[a flexed foot]* while he strikes his heels to sound his bells, and when both heels are tapped as in frappe *[stamp]* talons *[heels]* the position is tantamount to pieds joints *[feet together]* (Arbeau, M.S. Evans, trans., p. 178).

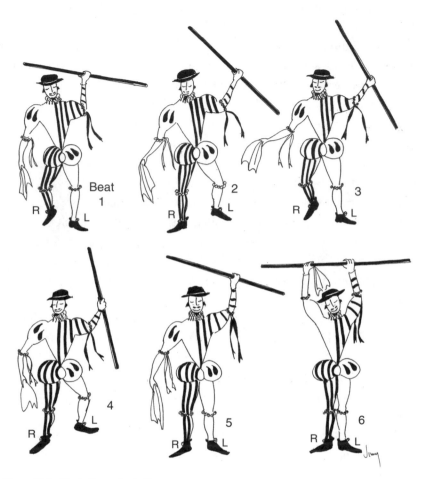

Figure 11.2   Morris Dance Basic Step

MORRIS DANCE

Set for Keyboard by
Michael Sebastian

Musical Example 11.1   Morris Dance

In other words:

1st beat: stamp left heel (frappe talon gauche)
2nd beat: stamp right heel (frappe talon droit)
3rd beat: stamp left heel (frappe talon gauche)
4th beat: stamp right heel (frappe talon droit)
5th beat: stamp both heels (frappe talons)
6th beat: pause with feet together

This repeats throughout the dance, with the patterns moving forward, back, and to the side. Kicks, jumps, clicking of sticks, and clashing of swords were also incorporated into these movements. William Kemp, the Shakespearean comic, once jogged the Morris dance with his bells from London to Norwich in gratitude for the favors his career had brought him. Lincoln Kirstein said that Morris dancing was much more fun to do than to watch. Arbeau said the dance gave you the gout. Who knew?

Figure 12.1 Roundel (the Witches in *Macbeth*)

CHAPTER 12
ROUNDEL/RINGLET

MACBETH

Act IV, scene i

FIRST WITCH: Ay, sir, all this is so. But why
Stands Macbeth thus amazedly?
Come, sisters, cheer we up his sprites
And show the best of our delights.
I'll charm the air to give a sound
While you perform your antic ROUND[1],
That this great king may kindly say
Our duties did this welcome pay.
[Music. The Witches dance, and vanish.]

---

[1]Antic Round: Grotesque circular dance. A. Harbage, ed. *Macbeth.* In A. Harbage, ed., *The Complete Pelican Shakespeare.* Baltimore: Penguin Books, 1969.

A MIDSUMMER NIGHT'S DREAM

Act II, scene ii

[Enter Titania, Queen of Fairies, with her Train]
TITANIA: Come, now a ROUNDEL[2] and a fairy song;
Then, for the third part of a minute, hence—
Some to kill cankers in the musk-rose bud
Some war with reremice for their leathern wings,
To make my small elves coats, and some keep back
The clamorous owl, that nightly hoots and wonders
At our quaint spirits. Sing me now asleep.
Then to your offices, and let me rest.
[Fairies sing]

FIRST FAIRY: You spotted snakes with double tongue,
Thorney hedgehogs, be not seen;
Newts and blindworms, do no wrong
Come not near our Fairy Queen.
[Chorus]
Philomele, with melody
Sing in our sweet lullaby,
Lulla, lulla, lullaby; lulla, lulla, lullaby;
Never harm
Nor spell nor charm
Come our lovely lady nigh.
So good night, with lullaby.

FIRST FAIRY: Weaving spiders, come not here:
Hence, you long-legged spinners, hence!
Beetles black, approach not near;
Worm nor snail, do no offense.
[Chorus] Philomele, with melody, &c. [She sleeps.]
SECOND FAIRY: Hence, away! Now all is well.
One aloof stand sentinel.
[Exeunt Fairies]

---

[2]Roundel ('raundl) ronde; a refrain; dance: ronde. *Langenscheidt's Standard Dictionary.*

Act II, scene i

TITANIA: These are the forgeries of jealousy;
And never, since the middle summer's spring,
Met we on a hill, in dale, forest, or mead,
Be paved fountain or by rushy brook,
Or in the beached margent of the sea,
To dance our RINGLETS[3] to the whistling wind,
But with thy brawls thou hast disturbed our sport.
Therefore the winds, piping to us in vain,
As in revenge, have sucked up from the sea
Contagious fogs; which falling in the land
Hath every pelting river made so proud
That they have overborne their continents.
The ox hath therefore stretched his yoke in vain,
The ploughman lost his sweat, and the green corn
Hath rotted ere his youth attained a beard;
The fold stands empty in the drowned field,
And crows are fatted with the murrion flock;
The nine men's morris is filled up with mud;
And the quaint mazes in the wanton green
For lack of tread are undistinguishable.
The human mortals want their winter here;
No night is now with hymn or carol blest.
Therefore the moon, the governess of floods,
Pale in her anger, washes all in air,
That rheumatic diseases do abound.
And thorough this distemperature we see
The seasons alter: hoary-headed frosts
Fall in the fresh lap of the crimson rose,
And on old Hiems' thin and icy crown
An odorous chaplet of sweet summer buds
Is, as in mockery, set. The spring, the summer,
The chilling autumn, angry winter change
Their wonted liveries; and the mazed world,
By their increase, now knows not which is which.

---

[3]Ringlets: Dances in a ring. M. Doran, ed. *A Midsummer Night's Dream.* In A. Harbage, ed., *The Complete Pelican Shakespear.* Baltimore: Penguin Books, 1969.

And this same progeny of evil comes
From our debate, from our dissension;
We are their parents and original.

Act II, scene i

OBERON: How long within this wood intend you stay?

TITANIA: Perchance till after Theseus' wedding day.
If you will patiently dance in our ROUND[4]
And see our moonlight revels, go with us.
If not, shun me, and I will spare your haunts.

The earliest dance form is the circle. People have danced around everything—from sacrificial fires to maypoles—and each other since civilization began. It is the easiest way to move around something and maintain a rhythmic beat. Processional lines, serpentine lines all eventually end up in a circle as the dance proceeds. The rhythms change according to the specific dance—step-hop, kick-hop, run, glide, jump, or it can vary with different sequences: changing directions, changing partners, any combination the choreographer cares to create in order to build the patterns to the climax of the dance.

The Witches in *Macbeth* dance around the cauldron. The fairies and Titania dance in a circle to bless the forest in *A Midsummer Night's Dream*. And the Shapes dance around the banquet table in *The Tempest*. Circle dances are very easy to execute: Just face center, join hands (or not), and take off using any step the choreographer designs to fit the rhythms or melody of the piece.

---

[4]Round: Round dance. M. Doran, ed. *A Midsummer Night's Dream*. In A. Harbage, ed., *The Complete Pelican Shakespeare*. Baltimore: Penguin Books, 1969.

ROUNDEL

BOURREE I, Suite III in C Major

J.S. Bach

Musical Example 12.1   Roundel

Figure A 1   Waltz

Appendix 1
Other Social Dances

The periods or eras in which a director may place his Shakespearean production and the possible dances that could be substituted for the dances of Shakespeare are noted here. Each era had many many dances that became popular. Few sustained a long run. The most known from each era and a few that are not so well known but that are fun to do are listed here also.

The Periods

Greek/Roman (500 to 100 B.C.), Medieval/Middle Ages/Early Tudor (1100 to 1500), Renaissance/Elizabethan/Jacobean (1550 to 1640), Restoration/Baroque (1660 to 1700), Empire/Rococo (1700 to 1800), Romantic (1780 to 1840), Victorian/Edwardian (1840 to 1910), and Modern (1910 to the present).

Through the 1980s and 1990s, traditional social dances began to lose their distinction. The waltz, polka, fox-trot, jitterbug, tango, and cha-cha have remained popular since their introduction and are still danced in ballrooms and at weddings and other social gatherings. The novelty dances, on the other hand, fell by the wayside as others took their place. Dancing became more and more generic as the dancers began to mix the styles. Then break-dancing and hip-hop, which came from the streets, developed their own styles, and emerged as the core of the choreography seen on MTV and in modern musical presentations. Add the discipline of jazz and classical ballet to that mix, and you're in for some very exciting dancing. There are dance halls today that feature specific styles of dance. In the western clubs the one-step and two-step are danced, as well as line dancing. The Latin dances of the 1950s have been kept alive by salsa. Latin dancing keeps reinventing itself with the exciting music of Reggaeton and the Spanish hip-hop. There are also clubs for swing dancing. These dances follow specific steps, but their structure allows for improvisation.

People today get on the dance floor and improvise to the music, having never been taught the dance steps or style of a particular dance. They move to the music. In a social situation, this gives the dancers a wonderful freedom and is great fun. This is also how new social dances are created. In Shakespeare's time they had great fun, too, but the dances at court were very specific in style and steps, having been honed by the dancing masters. There was room for improvisation, but it was done on musical cue as in the galliard. The court dancing was ruled by the dancing masters and the propriety of the time. Many of the dances enacted at court had their beginings in country dancing. But these dances also had rules. See John Playford's book, *The English Dancing Master*, written in 1651.

Here are some comparable dances from other periods that fit the mood and style of the dances in Shakespeare's text.

Greek/Roman (500 to 100 B.C.)

Line Dances—A single-file serpentine dance stepping to every beat of the music.

Round Dances—A dance circling in a clockwise or counterclockwise movement and stepping to every beat of music.

Fertility Dances—Dances that are performed in a circular movement around an object such as a maypole or any other symbol of regeneration.

Medieval/Middle Ages/Early Tudor (1100 to 1550)

Basse Danse—A dance where the steps were kept low to the floor as opposed to the "haute danse," which used hops and jumps. It incorporates the branle in its structure and is danced in 3/4 time.

Farandole—A skip-hop line dance in 6/8 time.

Folk Dances—Couple dances, as in barn dancing, in 4/4 time.

Jig—A dance danced with or without a partner in 6/8, 9/9, or 12/8 time.

Morris Dance—A dance involving six to nine individual dancers working with props in 4/4 time.

Renaissance/Elizabethan/Jacobean (1550 to 1640)

These dances can be found in previous chapters.

Restoration/Baroque (1660 to 1700)

Gavotte—A lively folk dance in 4/4 time. Later it became a stately dance.

Coranto—A running dance in 3/4 time.

Cotillion—A square dance in 4/4 time.

Minuet—A slow dance from the French court using small steps in various patterns. It is danced in 3/4 time.

Empire/Rococo (1700 to 1800)

Flamenco—A passionate dance with castanets, heel drumming, and "olé" shouting.

The coranto, jig, gavotte, and minuet remained popular.

Romantic (1780 to 1840)

Galop—A rapid gliding dance in 2/4 time.

Mazurka—A round dance in 3/4 time with an accented heel tap on the second beat.

Polka—A hop-skip dance in 2/4 time.

Quadrille—A square dance for four couples. Originally performed on horseback.

Schottische—A dance involving turns alternating with hopping, gliding steps to polka music.

Waltz—A couple dance that revolves around the ballroom with the man holding the woman in the ballroom dance position that is used today. The dance is in 3/4 time, which became known as waltz time. The Viennese waltz is very fast in tempo. The Chekovian waltz accents the second beat. Later, the waltz was tamed to a box step danced in place.

Victorian/Edwardian (1840 to 1910)

Cakewalk—A strutting, kicking dance in 2/4 time.
Reels—A gliding couple dance in 2/4 time.
Square Dances—Couples dancing in patterns called by a caller.
The galop, polka, waltz, and the schottische remained popular.

Modern

1910 to 1920

Animal Dances—bunny hug, buzzard lope, camel walk, eagle rock, grizzly bear, kangaroo dip, and turkey trot, to name a few—The dances were danced by partners impersonating the animal for which the dance was named. Danced in 2/4 or 4/4 time.
Fox-Trot—The original consisted of two gliding steps and seven quick steps in 2/4 or 4/4 time.
Maxixe—A rhythmic lilting dance danced forward and back in 2/4 time.
One-Step—A dance that steps on every beat; also known as the turkey trot.
Tango—A seductive dance from Argentina with intricate footwork danced in 2/4 time.
The polka and the waltz remained popular.

1920 to 1930

Black Bottom—A very risque native dance featuring slapping of the backside while hopping forward and back, jumping, stamping, and gyrating the pelvis. Danced in 2/4 time.
Ballin' the Jack—"First you put your two feet close up tight then you sway them to the left then you sway them to the right. Step around the floor kinda nice and light then you twist around and twist around with all your might. Spread your lovin' arms way out in space you do the 'Eagle Rock' with style and grace. Put right foot out and then you bring it back and that's what I call 'Ballin' The Jack.'

Danced in 4/4 time. Words by Jim (James Henry) Burris; music by Chris Smith.

Charleston—An up-and-down movement with changing footwork and sidekicks danced in 2/2 time.

English Quickstep—A fast fox-trot danced with gliding turning steps in 2/4 time.

Fox-Trot—A trotting box step danced in 2/4 or 4/4 time.

Lindy Hop—The forerunner of the jitterbug, featuring improvised steps danced in 4/4 time.

Rumba—A hip-swaying elegant dance from Cuba danced in 2/4 or 4/4 time.

Shimmy—A dance that involves standing still and vibrating in 2/4 time.

Varsity Drag—A dance from the show "Good News" by Bud DeSylva, Lew Brown, and Ray Henderson (1927): "Down on your heels up on your toes. Stay after school, see how it goes. That's the way to do the Varsity Drag" in 2/4 time.

The polka, tango and waltz remained popular.

1930 to 1940

Beguine—A slow, swaying Latin dance in 4/4 time.

Conga—A serpentine line dance involving holding onto the waist of the person in front of you and stepping 1-2-3-kick. Danced to Latin music in 4/4 time.

Fox-Trot—A slowed-down version of the original. Danced in "slows" and "quicks," in 4/4 time. Still popular today.

Jitterbug—A very energetic couple dance incorporating lifts and breaking apart from time to time. Danced in 4/4 time.

Paso Doble—A Spanish one-step emulating the bull fights.

Samba—A lilting pendulum dance from Rio danced in 2/4 time.

The polka, rumba, tango, fox-trot, and waltz remained popular.

1940 to 1950

Fox-Trot—A medium tempo dance in 4/4 time.

The conga, jitterbug, rumba, samba, tango, and waltz remained popular.

Figure A 2   Polka

1950 to 1960

Hokey-Pokey—A circle dance following the words of the song by
Roland Lawrence LaPrise, "You put your left foot in. You pull your
left foot out. You put your left in and you shake it all about. You do
the Hokey-Pokey and you turn yourself about. And that's what it's
all about." The song has endless verses. Danced in 4/4 time.

Bunny Hop—A line dance that involves taking and stepping the waist
of the person in front of you: heel-toe, heel-toe on left; heel-toe,
heel-toe on right; Hop forward, hop back, hop forward three times.
It is repeated over and over around the ballroom in 4/4 time.

Cha-Cha—A syncopated step forward and back. Danced together or
apart to a Latin beat accenting the second beat of the measure.
Danced in 4/4 time.

Mambo—A rapid Latin dance accenting the 4th beat of the measure in 4/4 time.

Merengue—A Latin dance with a side step to the left that drags the right foot, causing a limp with a hip movement. Danced in 2/4 time.

St. Louis Shag—A shuffling, kicking, hopping dance in 4/4 time.

Stroll—A line dance similar to the camel walk, danced to a slow rock beat in 4/4 time.

Twist—A dance, made made popular by Chubby Checker, that involves standing in place, shifting your weight, and twisting your hips side to side in 4/4 time.

The fox-trot, jitterbug, rumba, samba, tango, and waltz remained popular.

1960 to 1970

Bossa Nova—A popular dance combining the Brazilian samba with American jazz. Danced in 2/4 time.

Any of the novelty dances that are in 2/4 or 4/4 time, namely, the frug, hitch hike, hully-gully, jerk, pony, and swim. They are all stationary with a lot of hip and arm action.

The cha-cha, fox-trot, jitterbug, tango, and waltz remained popular.

1970 to present

The same as in the previous decade. It is fortunate that the Latin dances, country dances, and traditional ballroom dances are kept very much alive today by interested people. Rap moves, hip-hop, and other popular dances of today should not be discounted.

The following section includes lists of dances, modern and ancient, that are comparable in mood and tempo to the dances Shakespeare mentions in his plays.

THE BERGOMASK (Chapter 3)
Greek/Roman (500 to 100 B.C.)

Line Dances
Round Dances
Fertility Dances

Medieval/Middle Ages/Early Tudor (1100 to 1550)

Farandole
Folk Dances
Morris Dance

Renaissance/Elizabethan/Jacobean (1550 to 1640)

Bergomask

Restoration/Baroque (1660 to 1700)

Gavotte (before it was made a stately dance by the court)
Coranto
Cotillion

Empire/Rococo (1700 to 1800)

Coranto
Cotillion
Jig

Romantic (1780 to 1840)

Galop
Polka
Schottische

Victorian/Edwardian (1840 to 1910)

Cakewalk
Reels
Square Dances
Galop
Polka

Modern (1910 to 1920)

Animal Dances
Square Dances
Polka

1920 to 1930

Black Bottom
Charleston
Lindy Hop
Varsity Drag

1930 to 1940

Conga
Hokey-Pokey
Jitterbug

1940 to 1950

Conga
Jitterbug
Square Dances

1950 to 1960

Bunny Hop
St. Louis Shag
Twist

1960 to 1970

Frug
Hitch Hike
Jerk
Swim

1970 to present

Jitterbug
Square Dances
Any of the novelty dances from the past decades.

THE BRAWL (BRANLE/HAY) (Chapter 4)

Greek/Roman (500 to 100 B.C.]

Round Dances

Medieval/Middle Ages/Early Tudor (1100 to 1550)

Basse Danse
Branle
Round Dances

Renaissance/Elizabethan/Jacobean (1550 to 1640)

Brawl/Branle

Restoration/Baroque (1660 to 1700)

Minuet

Empire/Rococo (1700 to 1800)

Minuet

Romantic (1780 to 1840)

Waltz

Victorian/Edwardian (1840 to 1910)

Reels
Round Dances
Waltz

Modern (1910 to 1920)

Tango
Waltz

Figure A 3   Tango

1920 to 1930

Rumba
Tango
Waltz

1930 to 1940

Beguine
Rumba
Tango
Waltz

1940 to 1950

Fox Trot
Tango
Waltz

1950 to 1960

Cha-Cha
Fox-Trot
Rumba
Stroll
Waltz

1960 to 1970

Bossa Nova
Cha-Cha
Fox-Trot
Tango
Waltz

1970 to present

Any of the dances from the last decade can be used. The music of today would work as long as it is an easy 4/4 beat.

THE CANARY (Chapter 5)

Greek/Roman (500 to 100 B.C.)

Round Dances
Fertility Dances

Medieval/Middle Ages/Early Tudor (1100 to 1550)

Jig
Morris Dance

Renaissance/Elizabethan/Jacobean (1550 to 1640)

Canary

Restoration/Baroque (1660 to 1700)

Cotillion
Minuet

Empire/Rococo (1700 to 1800)

Flamenco
Minuet

Romantic (1780 to 1840)

Mazurka

Victorian/Edwardian (1840 to 1910)

Galop
Reels

Modern (1910 to 1920)

Maxixe
One-Step
Tango

1920 to 1930

English Quickstep
Rumba
Tango

1930 to 1940

Conga
Samba
Rumba
Tango

Figure A 4   Rumba

1940 to 1950

Conga
Rumba
Samba
Tango

1950 to 1960

Cha-Cha
Mambo
Merengue
Tango

1960 to 1970

Cha-Cha
Mambo
Tango

1970 to present

Any dance with an exotic beat. The flamenco, mazurka, or paso doble could be used.

THE CORANTO/COURANTE (Chapter 6)

Greek/Roman (500 to 100 B.C.)

Line Dances
Round Dances

Medieval/Middle Ages/Early Tudor (1100 to 1550)

Folk Dances
Jig

Renaissance/Elizabethan/Jacobean (1550 to 1640)

Coranto

Restoration/Baroque (1660 1700)

Coranto
Cotillion

Empire/Rococo (1700 to 1800)

Coranto
Jig

Romantic (1780 to 1840)

Galop
Polka
Schottische
Waltz (Viennese)

Victorian/Edwardian (1840 to 1910)

Galop
Polka
Reels
Waltz

Modern (1910 to 1920)

One-Step
Tango
Waltz

1920 to 1930

English Quickstep
Fox-Trot
Polka
Tango
Waltz

1930 to 1940

Fox-Trot
Polka
Tango
Waltz

1940 to 1950

Fox Trot
Jitterbug
Polka
Samba
Waltz

1950 to 1960

Cha-Cha
Fox-Trot
Jitterbug
Mambo

1960 to 1970

Bossa Nova
Cha-Cha
Fox-Trot

1970 to present

Stay with the partner dances as the coranto was danced in couples moving about the dance hall.

THE GALLIARD (Chapter 7)

Greek/Roman (500 to 100 B.C.)

Line Dances
Round Dances

Medieval/Middle Ages/Early Tudor (1100 to 1550)

Folk Dances
Jig
Morris Dance

Renaissance/Elizabethan/Jacobean (1550 to 1640)

Galliard
La Volta

Restoration/Baroque (1660 to 1700)

Gavotte (early)
Coranto
Cotillion
Jig

Empire/Rococo (1700 to 1800)

Coranto
Jig

Romantic (1780 to 1840)

Galop
Quadrille

Victorian/Edwardian (1840 to 1910)

Cakewalk
Galop
Reel

Modern (1910 to 1920)

The most physical of the animal dances

1920 to 1930

Black Bottom
Charleston

1930 to 1940

Jitterbug

1950 to 1960

Jitterbug
St. Louis Shag

1960 to 1970

Any of the solo novelty dances danced in the discotheques. The wilder the better.

1970 to present

Anything from the discotheques to break-dancing to hip-hop.

THE JIG (GIGUE) (Chapter 8)
Greek/Roman (500 to 100 B.C.)

Line Dances
Round Dances

Medieval/Middle Ages/Early Tudor (1100 to 1550)

Morris Dance

Renaissance/Elizabethan/Jacobean (1550 to 1640)

Jig

Restoration/Baroque (1660 to 1700)

Coranto
Jig

Empire/Rococo (1700 to 1800)

Coranto
Jig

Romantic (1780 to 1800)

Galop
Jig
Polka

Victorian/Edwardian (1840 to 1910)

Galop
Jig
Polka
Reel

Modern (1910 to 1920)

Animal Dances
Jig
Polka

1920 to 1930

Black Bottom
Charleston
Jig
Shimmy

1930 to 1940

Hokey-Pokey
Jitterbug

1940 to 1950

Jitterbug
Jig

1950 to 1960

Bunny Hop
Jitterbug
Jig

1960 to 1970

Frug
Hitch Hike
Jerk
Jitterbug
Jig
Pony

1970 to present

The dances from the discotheques.
Jitterbug
Jig

LA VOLTA (Chapter 9)

Greek/Roman (500 to 100 B.C.)

Line Dances
Round Dances
Fertility Dances

Medieval/Middle Ages/Early Tudor (1100 to 1550)

Line Dances
Round Dances
Morris Dance

Figure A 5   Jitterbug

Renaissance/Elizabethan/Jacobean (1550 to 1640)

La Volta
Galliard

Restoration/Baroque (1660 to 1700)

Coranto
Cotillion
Jig

Empire/Rococo (1700 to 1800)

Coranto
Jig

Romantic (1780 to 1840)

Galop
Mazurka

Victorian/Edwardian (1840 to 1910)

Cakewalk
Galop

Modern (1910 to 1920)

The more athletic animal dances
Polka (add a lift)

1920 to 1930

Charleston
Lindy Hop

1930 to 1940

Jitterbug
Lindy Hop

1940 to 1950

Jitterbug

1950 to 1960

Jitterbug
Mambo
St. Louis Shag

1960 to 1970

Jitterbug

1970 to present

Jitterbug

THE MEASURE/PAVAN (Chapter 10)

Greek/Roman (500 to 100 B.C.)

Line Dances
Round Dances

Medieval/Middle Ages/Early Tudor (1100 to 1550)

Basse Danse
Branle

Renaissance/Elizabethan/Jacobean (1550 to 1640)

Measure
Pavan

Restoration/Baroque (1660 to 1700)

Minuet

Empire/Rococo (1700 to 1800)

Minuet

Romantic (1780 to 1840)

Waltz

Victorian/Edwardian (1840 to 1910)

Reel
Waltz

Modern (1910 to 1920)

Tango
Waltz

1920 to 1930

Tango
Waltz

1930 to 1940

Beguine
Fox-Trot
Tango
Waltz

1940 to 1950

Fox-Trot
Rumba
Tango
Waltz

1950 to 1960

Fox-Trot
Rumba
Stroll
Tango
Waltz

Figure A 6   Hip-Hop

1960 to 1970

Bossa Nova
Fox-Trot
Waltz

1970 to present

Fox-Trot
Waltz

THE MORRIS DANCE and the ROUNDEL/RINGLET (Chapters 11 and 12)

The morris dance has remained popular and is danced in many festivals today. It can be used in all the periods from the Middle Ages to the present. In the Greek/Roman period (500 to 100 B.C.), it could be represented by fertility dances.

The roundel/ringlet is a round dance that be danced as such through all periods.

APPENDIX 2
THE PLAYS

The plays listed here merely call for "a dance" in the stage directions. I have made suggestions as to what specific dances could be danced in these scenes in Chapter 1.

The plays that call for a masque are listed below. They are discussed in Chapter 2.

Then there are plays in which specific dances are named in the text. They are covered in Chapters 3 through 12.

APPENDIX 3
THE MUSIC

The musical examples listed below are of the music played for dance at court, in the plays, masques, and country socials. According to Frederic V. Grunfeld in his book *Music* (p. 36), Shakespeare's musical comtemporaries were William Byrd, Thomas Morley, and John Bull. They all wrote pavans, voltas, galliards, and other dances.

The example used for the bergomask is actually an allemande. It is a lively piece of music in 3/4 time. The bergomask can be danced in 3/4 as well as 2/4 time, since the dancer steps to every beat of music. Both the allemande and bergomask were round dances of the sixteenth century. The musical examples used for the jig and roundel are from the seventeenth century.

REFERENCES

Arbeau, Thoinot. *Orchesography*. 1589. New translation by Mary Stuart Evans. New York: Dover, 1948.

Barker, Mary L. *Pears Cyclopaedia*. London: Pelham Books Ltd., 1968.

Benet, William Rose. *The Reader's Encyclopedia*. 2nd ed. London: Thomas Y. Crowell, 1969.

Blom, Eric, ed. *Grove's Dictionary of Music and Musicians*. New York. St. Martin's Press, 1966.

Briggs, Asa, consulting ed. *Everyday Life through the Ages*. London: Readers Digest, 1992.

Buckman, Peter. *Let's Dance*. New York and London: Paddington Press, 1978.

Caroso, Fabritio. *Courtly Dance of the Renaissance*. 1600. New translation and edition by Julia Sutton. New York: Dover, 1995.

Chute, Marchette. *Shakespeare of London*. E. P. Dutton & Co. Inc., 1949. Reprint, Book of the Month Club, Inc. U.S.A., 1996.

Craig, Hardin. *Shakespeare*. Palo Alto, CA: Scott, Foresman, 1931.

Collegium Terpsichore and Ulsamer Collegium. *Golden Dance Hits of 1600*. Archiv Produktion 2533 184. p1974.

Dolmetsch, Mabel. *Dances of England & France 1450 to 1600*. London: Routledge and Kegan Paul Ltd., 1949. Reprint, New York: Da Capo Press, Inc., 1976.

Dolmetsch, Mabel. *Dances of Spain and Italy from 1400 to 1600*. London: Routledge and Kegan Paul Ltd., 1954. Reprint, New York: Da Capo Press, Inc., 1975.

Emerson, Kathy Lynn. *Everyday Life in Renaissance England from 1485–1649*. Cincinnati, Ohio: Writer's Digest Books, 1996.

Gifford, William, ed. *The Works of Ben Jonson*. Boston: Phillips, Sampson, 1853.

Go Britannia! Travel Guide. Earth Mysteries: Morris Dancing. http://www.britannia.com/wonder/modance.html (accessed May 9, 2005).

Gove, Philop. B., ed. *Webster's Third New International Dictionary of the English Language, Unabridged*. Springfield, MA: Merriam, 1976.

Grunfeld, Frederic V. *Music*. New York: Newsweek Books, 1974.

Harbage, Alfred, gen. ed. *The Complete Pelican Shakespeare*. Baltimore: Penguin Books, 1969.

Harbage, Alfred, gen. ed. *William Shakespeare: The Complete Works*. New York: Viking Penguin, Inc., 1977.

Horst, Louis. *Pre-Classic Dance Forms*. Brooklyn, N.Y.: Dance Horizons, 1968.

Kirstein, Lincoln. *The Book of the Dance, A Short History of Classic Theatrical Dancing*. 1935. Reprint, Garden City, N.Y.: Garden City Publishing, 1942.

Kirstein, Lincoln. *The Classic Ballet*. New York: Alfred A. Knopf/Borzoi Books, 1952.

Kybalova, Ludmila, Olga Herbenova, and Milena Lamarova. *The Pictorial Encyclopedia of Fashion.* New York: Crown Publishers, Inc., 1968.

Manfull, Helen, and Lowell Manfull. *The Stage in Action.* Dubuque, Iowa: Kendall/Hunt Publishing, 1989.

McKay, David. *The Pocket Shakespeare in Thirteen Volumes.* Philadelphia: Author, n.d. (Available from David McKay, 1022 Market St., Philadelphia, Pa.)

Playford, John. *The English Dancing Master, or Plaine Easie Rules for the Dancing of Country Dances with the Tune to Each Dance.* 1651. Reprint, Alton, Hampshire, Great Britain: Dance Books Ltd., 1984.

Rolfe, Bari. *Movement for Period Plays.* Oakland, Calif.: Personabooks, 1985.

Russell, Douglas A. *Period Style for the Theatre.* Boston: Stanford University/Allyn and Bacon, Inc., 1980.

Strutt, Joseph. *The Sports and Pastimes of the People of England.* New York: A.M. Kelley, 1970.

StreetSwing.com Dance History Archives. Morris Dances. http://www.streetswing.com/histmain/z3moris.htm (accessed May 2, 2005).

Todd, Richard, Glynis Johns, James Robertson Justice, Michael Gough, and Jane Barrett. *The Sword and the Rose,* directed by Ken Annakin. Burbank, CA: Walt Disney Home Video, 1997.

Urwin, Kenneth, ed. *Langenscheidt's Standard French Dictionary. French-English, English-French.* Berlin and Munich: Langenscheidt KG, 1988.

Wallace, Carol, Don McDonagh, Jean L. Dreusedow, Laurence Libin, and Constance Old. *Dance, a Very Social History.* New York: The Metropolitan Museum of Art and Rizzoli International Publications, Inc., 1986.

Whiting, Leonard, Olivia Hussey, Milo O Shea, and Michael York. *Romeo and Juliet,* directed by Franco Zeffirelli. VHS/DVD. Hollywood, CA: Paramount Studios, 1968.

Wood, Melusine. *Historical Dances 12th to 19th Century.* London: Imperial Society of Teachers of Dancing, 1972.

Zorn, Friedrich A. *Grammar of the Art of Dancing.* tr. Alfon, J. Sheafe. Boston: Heintzemann Press 1905. Reprint, Brooklyn, N.Y.: Dance Horizons, 1975.

INDEX

Note: Illustrations are listed in italics